Accounting Fundamentals
for
Nonfinancial Executives

Allen Sweeny

Accounting Fundamentals
for
Nonfinancial Executives

American Management Association, Inc.

International standard book number: 0-8144-5286-8
Library of Congress catalog card number: 78-173320
Second printing

To
Petrea

Preface

THE field of basic accounting frankly offers little that is new or exciting in terms of content. Literally hundreds of books have been written on the subject, and this one makes no pretense of breaking new ground. It has, however, been written with definite, if more modest, purposes: first, to simplify basic accounting (and some financial) concepts and, second, to present these ideas as briefly and clearly as possible.

Both these objectives assume that the reader is a non-financial executive with virtually no prior knowledge of accounting and—equally important—that he has neither the time nor the inclination to correct this situation. The nine concise chapters that follow attempt to provide a readable remedy that requires little time and effort.

This book presents several hypothetical personal situations to illustrate accounting concepts. Any similarity between the names used in these examples and those of any person, living or dead, is purely coincidental.

I am particularly grateful to Anne B. Ruscick, who, in her usual competent manner, found time to type, retype, and, in many other important ways, to assist in the preparation of this manuscript. My thanks also to Judith Finger of American Management Association for her editorial contributions.

Allen Sweeny

Contents

1

The Dual Aspect Principle

Aᴄᴄᴏᴜɴᴛɪɴɢ is frequently called the Language of Business. Undoubtedly many people feel that this particular description lends undue glamour to the often confusing and mysterious black art of bookkeeping. Still, the fact remains that accounting and finance are the primary tools for reducing business problems and opportunities to a common denominator, setting goals, measuring results, and making decisions.

An understanding of the basic concepts of accounting and finance is critical to the successful performance of every executive or businessman, whether he likes it or not. This book presents those concepts in as simple and straightforward a manner as possible. The following pages will certainly not train any accountants. Hopefully, however, they will help the busy nonfinancial executive to become knowledgeable about (1) fundamental accounting and financial concepts and practices, and (2) the uses, as

1

well as the limitations, of those practices in the managerial process.

To do this, we shall place more emphasis on concepts and essentials and less on explanations of debits, credits, and ledgers, since our purpose is to explain how to use, rather than how to create, financial data. More important, we shall concentrate on the inherently commonsensical aspects of the accounting and financial function. In adopting this approach, there is no intent to downgrade the exacting and critical role of the professional accountant. Nor should the reader assume that the accounting and financial transactions of large and complex business organizations are always simple. The point, rather, is that the basic concepts which underlie the accounting function are the keys to understanding it and are often amazingly simple.

To explore these propositions more specifically, let's begin with the two concepts that are at the heart of all accounting theory and practice. This chapter will deal with the first of those, the dual aspect principle; Chapter 2 will discuss the second, the accrual concept.

Let's illustrate the dual aspect with a hypothetical but common personal situation, the purchase of a home. This activity involves the screening and then the selection of the house to be bought. (Somewhere in the process, several near divorces are likely to occur.) Finally, the necessary financing must be arranged. Assume that the house can be purchased for $40,000 and that to make this purchase, we wish to borrow $30,000, which is to be financed through a conventional 25-year mortgage loan.

The rub, of course, is that we must convince some friendly banker of our credit worthiness. To evaluate our credit standing, he will want to know whether we can make the necessary down payment on the house and then repay the mortgage loan with interest over the next 25 years. In other words, he wants to know what we're worth. The process to determine this information is not especially complex.

First, he will want to know what things of value we own and how much money we owe and to whom. Assume that our response to these questions looks like this:

Things of Value		*Amount Owed*	
Cash		Personal bank loan	$2,000
Checking account	$ 500		
Savings	5,500		
Stock at current			
market value	8,000		
Total	$14,000		

For the sake of brevity, assume that our personal financial situation meets with approval, and that we (along with our friendly banker) now become happy homeowners. As a result of this transaction our financial situation now looks like this:

Things of Value		*Amounts Owed*	
Cash			
Checking account	$ 500		
Stock	3,500	Personal bank loan	$ 2,000
House	40,000	25-year mortgage loan	30,000
Total	$44,000	Total	$32,000

Through this simple and familiar process, we have not only become homeowners but have also made use of some key accounting concepts. For example, one of the basic facts in which our banker was interested was what things of value we owned. The same question could be phrased:

What are your assets? "Assets" is the word accountants use to describe things of value. Others, of course, also use this term, but the accountant uses it to describe something of value measurable in monetary terms. This approach was used in our bank application. Therefore, even if we are possessed of excellent health, good looks, and a dynamic personality, these assets—no matter how valuable—are not readily measurable in monetary terms and were not listed as assets in our loan application.

We were also asked to list what we owed and to whom. In general as well as in accounting terminology, such obligations are referred to as "liabilities" and represent a legal commitment. To be legally obligated is, in fact, to be liable. Another way to think of liabilities is as a claim on our assets. The person to whom we are liable has a claim on our assets up to the amount of credit he had extended to us. Another word for a claim such as this is "equity." Special courts, called "courts of equity," specialize in the just and impartial settlement of contending claims. In our particular illustration, our creditor (the bank) extended to us a personal loan of $2,000, and we were liable to him for a claim on assets in this amount. In this case and all others, the claim of the creditor on these assets is a liability.

If this liability is $2,000, there are obviously still $12,000 of assets to be claimed, and the next logical question is: Who has a claim on these? If no other creditors have a claim on these assets, obviously we, the owner, have a claim on them, and they are called "owner's equity." Thus there can be two types of equities (claims against our assets)—liabilities, or claims of lendors or creditors, and owner's equity, or claims of the owners.

In terms of assets, liabilities, and equities, the financial information on the loan application before and after purchase would appear as follows:

BEFORE PURCHASE

Assets		*Equities*	
Cash			
Checking account	$ 500		
Savings	5,500	Liabilities	
Stock at current		Personal loan	$ 2,000
market value	8,000	Owner's equity	12,000
Total assets	$14,000	Total equities	$14,000

AFTER PURCHASE

Assets		*Equities*	
Cash			
Checking account	$ 500	Personal loan	$ 2,000
Stock	3,500	Mortgage loan	30,000
House	40,000	Owner's equities	12,000
Total assets	$44,000	Total liabilities and owner's equities	$44,000

We can see by comparing these tables that although we now own a home, our personal, or owner's, equity remains unchanged after the purchase. The reason is that although our assets increased, a corresponding increase occurred in the creditor's claim on those assets.

Consider an additional point. We have said that two groups can have claims on assets—creditors and owners. Creditors are legally entitled to the first claim, and the balance that remains is the owner's equity. Thus, neither the creditors, nor the owners, nor the two groups together can have total claims on the assets that are in excess of the *total* assets. We come, therefore, to the observation that *assets must always equal equities,* or (since equities may take the form of liabilities and also owner's equity), *assets must also always equal liabilities plus owner's equity.*

The fact that assets equal equities is the basic principle of all accounting theory and practice. It is often referred to as the basic accounting equation, and is sometimes called the "dual aspect principle." Accounting systems are based on the inherent logic of this principle. Thus all business transactions are recorded in terms of their dual effect on assets and equities.

Our illustration involved a single business transaction—the purchase of a home. The two aspects of this transaction were:

1. To show an increase in our assets in the amount of $30,000, with an equal increase in equities (creditor's equities) in the same amount. (All accounting systems based on the dual aspect principle are of necessity described as "double-entry bookkeeping systems.")
2. To point out in general terms three basic concepts: assets as things of measurable monetary value; liabilities as creditor's claims against assets; and owner's equities as the claims of owners on assets.

Let's take these same concepts and, using exactly the same approach, see how they apply in a highly simplified business situation involving Gerry Manero's Furniture Mart.

After working for many years as head salesman for a

local furniture manufacturer, Gerry has decided to open his own furniture store. To do this, he plans to use his personal cash savings in the amount of $15,000. If Gerry goes into business on July 27, 1971, his accountant, using the foregoing concepts, will describe the balance of Gerry's assets and equities as follows:

GERRY MANERO'S FURNITURE MART
Balance of Assets and Equities
July 27, 1971

Assets		*Equities*	
Cash	$15,000	Owner's equity	$15,000

If, on July 30, Gerry purchases a delivery truck, the accountant will show this revised situation as follows:

GERRY MANERO'S FURNITURE MART
Balance of Assets and Equities
July 30, 1971

Assets		*Equities*	
Cash	$10,000	Owner's equities	$15,000
Delivery truck	5,000		
Total assets	$15,000		

Similarly, a decision executed a week later to obtain a $5,000 loan will prompt the accountant to reflect another change in Gerry's financial situation:

GERRY MANERO'S FURNITURE MART
Balance of Assets and Equities
August 6, 1971

Assets		*Equities*	
		Liabilities	
Cash	$15,000	Bank loan	$ 5,000
Truck	5,000	Owner's equity	15,000
Total assets	$20,000	Total equities	$20,000

We'll return to Gerry's entrepreneurial endeavor, but for the moment let's examine what the accountant has done to this point. By applying the same concepts we used in our home purchase illustration, he has prepared a financial evaluation of Gerry's new business on July 27, July 30, and August 6. This evaluation, like the loan application in our illustration, represents the balance of the assets and equities of the business as it stood on these dates.

In accounting, such a statement is called a "Balance Sheet." It is one of two basic accounting documents used to report on the financial condition of a company. Its name is well chosen, since it (1) always shows a balance of assets and equities, and (2) must always balance assets and equities, as we've already seen from the dual aspect concept.

Under normal business circumstances, the balance of assets and equities being reported in a Balance Sheet is constantly changing. For example, each of the three Balance Sheets shown for the furniture mart is different from the others as a result of the business Gerry Manero transacts on each of those days. To put it another way, the asset cash in almost any company is something that will change several times during one day or even within one hour.

Thus a Balance Sheet can reflect the status of assets and equities only at a given moment. For this reason, the Balance Sheet is always dated, and that date is critical to a clear understanding of the financial information being presented.

Most companies usually prepare a formal Balance Sheet at least once annually, usually as of the end of the year. Clearly, the elementary nature of Gerry Manero's financial affairs simplifies the preparation of a Balance Sheet in his business; the fact remains, however, that the same basic concepts are used no matter what the size or complexity of the business.

For example, Exhibit 1 shows the Balance Sheet of another GM—not Gerry Manero but rather General Motors, one of the world's largest industrial organizations.

Looking at the GM Balance Sheet, we note the prominence of its date, which indicates the exact day of the status report on the company's assets and equities. Next, note that the left-hand side of the statement lists the assets owned by the corporation. (Some or all of the various technical classifications of assets, liabilities, and equities shown on the GM Balance Sheet may be unfamiliar to the reader. At this point we can ignore that fact, for we are looking at Balance Sheets in very broad conceptual terms and will present a more detailed discussion of their makeup in Chapter 3.)

The right-hand side of the statement lists the claims on the company's assets. As we have seen in the two simpler cases, these are the claims of the creditors, or the liabilities. (There are also a series of claims called "reserves" which in this instance, as is many others, represent claims on assets that can be made by employees as a result of benefit payments which the company is legally committed to pay.) The final section on the right is entitled "stockholders' equity." GM is a corporation, so this is another way of representing the owner's equity.

The size and complexity of the assets, liabilities, and equities of a company may vary, but the basic concepts involved in preparing a Balance Sheet for them remain unchanged—and simple.

Exhibit 1. General Motors Balance Sheet, December 31, 1970.

ASSETS — DECEMBER 31, 1970

	Dec. 31, 1970
CURRENT ASSETS	
Cash	$ 323,243,635
United States and other government securities and time deposits—at cost, which approximates market	70,854,903
Accounts and notes receivable (less allowances)	1,725,665,981
Inventories—at the lower of cost (substantially first-in, first-out or average) or market	4,115,060,497
TOTAL CURRENT ASSETS.................................	6,234,825,016
INVESTMENTS AND MISCELLANEOUS ASSETS	
Investments in subsidiary companies not consolidated—at equity in net assets	984,436,185
United States Government securities maturing 1972—at cost	40,290,721
Other investments and miscellaneous assets—at cost (less allowances)...	60,984,047
TOTAL INVESTMENTS AND MISCELLANEOUS ASSETS	1,085,710,953
COMMON STOCK IN TREASURY — Available for Bonus Plan and Stock Option Plan (1970—1,529,045 shares; 1969—1,810,724 shares)	116,349,156
REAL ESTATE, PLANTS, AND EQUIPMENT	
Real estate, plants, and equipment—at cost	13,545,894,076
Less accumulated depreciation and obsolescence	8,132,437,359
Balance	5,413,456,717
Special tools—at cost less amortization	982,382,946
TOTAL REAL ESTATE, PLANTS, AND EQUIPMENT	6,395,839,663
PREPAID EXPENSES AND DEFERRED CHARGES......................	284,536,760
GOODWILL — Less amortization of $6,344,246 in 1970	57,098,219
TOTAL ASSETS	$14,174,359,767

LIABILITIES, RESERVES, AND STOCKHOLDERS' EQUITY — DECEMBER 31, 1970

	Dec. 31, 1970
CURRENT LIABILITIES	
Accounts payable	$ 1,659,892,993
United States and foreign income taxes	200,091,787
Other taxes, payrolls, and sundry accrued items	1,361,140,974
Dividends payable on preferred stocks	3,232,068
TOTAL CURRENT LIABILITIES	3,224,357,822
3¼% DEBENTURES DUE 1979 (less reacquired debentures in treasury: 1970—$122,528,000; 1969—$132,109,000)	35,522,000
FOREIGN DEBT OF SUBSIDIARIES DUE 1972-1992	245,700,700
OTHER LIABILITIES..	419,805,762
RESERVES	
Deferred investment tax credit	153,758,000
Contingent credits under Stock Option Plan	29,955,964
General reserve applicable to foreign operations	141,667,396
Other (principally unrealized intercompany profits)	69,821,501
TOTAL RESERVES..	395,202,861
STOCKHOLDERS' EQUITY	
Capital stock:	
Preferred, without par value (authorized, 6,000,000 shares):	
$5.00 series, stated value $100 per share, redeemable at $120 per share (issued, 1,875,366 shares; in treasury, 39,722 shares; outstanding, 1,835,644 shares)	183,564,400
$3.75 series, stated value $100 per share, redeemable at $101 per share (issued and outstanding, 1,000,000 shares)	100,000,000
Common, $1⅔ par value (authorized, 500,000,000 shares; issued, 287,586,179 shares at December 31, 1970 and 287,573,265 shares at December 31, 1969)	479,310,298
Total capital stock	762,874,698
Capital surplus (principally additional paid-in capital)	765,037,691
Net income retained for use in the business (earned surplus)	8,325,858,233
TOTAL STOCKHOLDERS' EQUITY..........................	9,853,770,622
TOTAL LIABILITIES, RESERVES, AND STOCKHOLDERS' EQUITY ..	$14,174,359,767

2

The Accrual Concept

Iɴ Chapter 1 we saw that the dual aspect principle is the conceptual touchstone of all accounting theory, but that it also has particular application to the preparation of one of the fundamental accounting statements, the Balance Sheet. In this chapter we will look at a second basic concept—the accrual principle—and examine its relationship to another basic accounting document, the Income Statement.

The accrual concept is a rather nettlesome notion, since most of us tend to conduct our personal financial affairs on a cash rather than an accrual basis. We tend to view our personal financial situation in light of how much cash or how many liquid assets we have on hand. Likewise, we think of our annual net income on a gross basis, or at best after taxes; we never, however, deduct the real depreciation on our automobile or the wear and tear associated with the use of household and personal effects. Depreciation will be discussed in Chapter 6; for now, let's return to Gerry Manero and continue to record the development of his new furniture mart. The initial three transactions described in Chapter 1 result in simplified Balance Sheets, as shown below.

Event: July 27. Gerry Manero decides to enter the furniture business and invests $15,000 of his personal savings.

GERRY MANERO'S FURNITURE MART
Balance Sheet
July 27, 1971

Assets		*Equity*	
Cash	$15,000	Owner's equity	$15,000

Event: July 30. Gerry Manero purchases a new delivery truck for his business.

GERRY MANERO'S FURNITURE MART
Balance Sheet
July 30, 1971

Assets		*Equity*	
Cash	$10,000	Owner's equity	$15,000
Delivery truck	5,000		
Total assets	$15,000		

Event: August 6. Gerry Manero obtains a $5,000 bank loan for his new business.

GERRY MANERO'S FURNITURE MART
Balance Sheet
August 6, 1971

Assets		*Equities*	
		Liabilities	
Cash	$15,000	Bank loan	$ 5,000
Delivery truck	5,000	Owner's equity	15,000
Total assets	$20,000	Total equities	$20,000

Let's continue this process with comments on the transactions that follow.

Event: September 6. Gerry Manero purchases merchandise to be resold, for $6,000, paying cash. (Merchandise that is purchased or manufactured by a business and held for eventual sale is called "inventory.")

GERRY MANERO'S FURNITURE MART
Balance Sheet
September 6, 1971

Assets		*Equities*	
Cash	$ 9,000	Liabilities	
Merchandise inventory	6,000	Bank loan	$ 5,000
Delivery truck	5,000	Owner's equity	15,000
Total assets	$20,000	Total equities	$20,000

Event: September 8. Gerry Manero sells merchandise for $600 in cash that cost $500.

Since this particular transaction presents a slightly new wrinkle involving Gerry's first sale (the exchange of goods for a price), let's follow its effect on the Balance Sheet step by step.

The effect on assets is relatively clear-cut. The cash asset increases from $9,000 to $9,600 as a result of cash received from the sale. On the other hand, inventory decreases by the amount of $500 (the cost of the merchandise sold). The other asset on the Balance Sheet, the truck, remains unchanged at $5,000. So, in total, Gerry Manero's assets now amount to $20,100:

Assets	
Cash	$ 9,600
Inventory	5,500
Truck	5,000
Total assets	$20,100

On the equity side of the Balance Sheet, the liability of a $5,000 loan, payable to the bank, remains unchanged. At first glance, owner's equity of $15,000 would also appear to remain the same. If this were the case, however, the total equities of $20,000 would be less than the assets of $20,100. We know this can't be correct, since the dual aspect concept states that assets must always equal equities. For the basic accounting equation to match, total equities must also equal $20,100. We can see why they should. The bank's claim of $5,000 on the assets has not changed. There are $15,100 of assets to be claimed, and these can now be claimed only by the owner. Gerry Manero's equity—that is, his owner's equity—has increased $100. The reason, of course, is that the $500 asset of merchandise was exchanged for another asset, cash of $600. All these changes result in a September 8 Balance Sheet that looks like this:

GERRY MANERO'S FURNITURE MART
Balance Sheet
September 8, 1971

Assets		Equities	
Cash	$ 9,600	Liabilities	
Merchandise inventory	5,500	Bank loan	$ 5,000
Delivery truck	5,000	Owner's equity	15,100
Total assets	$20,100	Total equities	$20,100

Event: September 10. Gerry Manero purchases $2,000 of merchandise and agrees to pay for it within sixty days.

The reader will recognize that in this transaction, Gerry Manero charges his purchase as we might charge a personal purchase at a department store. It represents a liability since we do not own the merchandise. This particular type of liability is called an "account payable" and appears on this Balance Sheet:

GERRY MANERO'S FURNITURE MART
Balance Sheet
September 10, 1971

Assets		*Equities*	
		Liabilities	
Cash	$ 9,600	Accounts payable	$ 2,000
Merchandise inventory	7,500	Bank loan	5,000
Delivery truck	5,000	Owner's equity	15,100
Total assets	$22,100	Total equities	$22,100

Event: September 12. Gerry Manero sells merchandise for $800 which cost $600. The customer agrees to pay the total amount in thirty days.

The reader will recognize that the effect of this transaction is the same as that which took place on September 8. The only difference is that instead of receiving cash outright, the furniture mart has received the promise of payment within thirty days. Although not cash, this promise represents an asset which is called an "account receivable." It appears in this Balance Sheet:

GERRY MANERO'S FURNITURE MART
Balance Sheet
September 12, 1971

Assets		*Equities*	
Cash	$ 9,600		
Accounts receivable	800	Liabilities	
Merchandise inventory	6,900	Accounts payable	$ 2,000
		Bank loan	5,000
Delivery truck	5,000	Owner's equity	15,300
Total assets	$22,300	Total equities	$22,300

Event: September 15. Gerry Manero sells $1,000 of merchandise which costs $700. The customer pays cash.

Here again, this transaction affects owner's equity in the same manner as the sales on September 10 and 12.

GERRY MANERO'S FURNITURE MART
Balance Sheet
September 15, 1971

Assets		*Equities*	
Cash	$10,600		
Accounts receivable	800	Liabilities	
		Accounts payable	$ 2,000
Merchandise inventory	6,200	Bank loan	5,000
Delivery truck	5,000	Owner's equity	15,600
Total assets	$22,600	Total equities	$22,600

Let's stop now to look at the following comparison of the original versus the last Balance Sheet for the furniture mart.

GERRY MANERO'S FURNITURE MART
Comparative Balance Sheet

Assets	*July 27*	*Sept. 15*	*Equities*	*July 27*	*Sept. 15*
Cash	$15,000	$10,600	Liabilities		
			Accounts payable		$ 2,000
Accounts receivable		800	Loan payable		5,000
Inventory		6,200	Subtotal		$ 7,000
Delivery truck		5,000	Owner's equity	$15,000	15,600
Total assets	$15,000	$22,600	Total equities	$15,000	$22,600

We note, first, that the furniture mart has increased its assets and equities by $5,600. Second, and more importantly, owner's equity, that is, Gerry Manero's equity, has increased $600. This occurred because the assets of merchandise were exchanged for another asset—cash—at a higher value. In accounting terms, such an increase in owner's equity is called "income" or "profit." It is important to remember that when the accountant refers to income, he is concerned exclusively with increases in owner's equity. Thus, on August 6, the furniture mart's total assets increased $5,000, but because liabilities simultaneously increased in the same amount, there was no change in owner's equity and, therefore, no income.

Actually, only two transactions of the furniture mart had an effect on owner's equity. These were the sales of merchandise on September 8 and 12. In the earlier sale, owner's equity increased at the same time cash increased because the customer paid money for his merchandise. On September 12, however, equity increased while cash remained unchanged because the customer bought the merchandise on credit. We can see that increases in owner's equity do not depend on increases or decreases in cash. Rather, owner's equity was changed in both cases because the monies obtained were greater than the costs of the goods sold.

These sales increased the owner's equity. In accounting, an increase in owner's equity is called "revenue." The process of turning the goods over to the customer, however, brought about a decrease in the owner's equity in the amount that was paid for the goods sold. This decrease in owner's equity is called an "expense." The difference between the revenue (an increase in owner's equity) and the expense (the decrease in owner's equity) is "net income."

The distinctive aspect of the two business transactions that affected owner's equity was not whether cash was increased or decreased but whether revenues were greater than expenses. The concept that net income is measured by increases or decreases in owner's equity rather than by increases or decreases in cash is called the "accrual concept."

The dual aspect concept has particular relevance to the accounting document of the Balance Sheet. The accrual concept is basic to the second fundamental accounting document, the Income Statement.

We can summarize our comments on the conceptual basis for an Income Statement as follows:

- In accounting, increases in owner's equity that arise from the sale and exchange of a good or service are called net income.
- When a business provides a good or service, the monies it receives increase owner's equity and are called revenues.
- The costs that business incurs to provide the good or service decrease the owner's equity and are called expenses.
- Under the accrual concept, net income is measured by the difference between revenues and expenses, *not* by increases or decreases in cash.

An Income Statement summarizes the revenues and expenses of a business over a given period of time and reflects the difference between the two as net income if revenues are greater than expenses. If expenses are greater than revenues, there has not been a net income to the owners, and the result is shown as a net loss.

A term that is often used interchangeably with "net income" is "profit." Thus an Income Statement is also referred to as a "Statement of Profit and/or Loss" (often abbreviated P/L Statement). The choice is only one of terminology, since the purpose and concept of the statement are the same under either label.

An Income Statement for Gerry Manero's Furniture Mart for the period between July 27 and September 15 would appear as follows:

GERRY MANERO'S FURNITURE MART
Income Statement
Period Ending September 15, 1971

Revenues	$2,400
Less cost of goods sold	1,800
Net income	$ 600

The source of these figures is as follows:

Revenues are increases to owner's equity through sales of merchandise:

September 8	$ 600
September 12	800
September 15	1,000
Total revenues as per income statement	$2,400

Expenses represent decreases to owner's equity for the costs associated with providing these goods:

September 8	$ 500
September 12	600
September 15	700
Total expenses as per income statement	$1,800

Revenues minus expenses equal net income, or $600, which is the net income to owner's equity for the period July 27 through September 15.

Our Income Statement shows the same net increase to

Suppose, for example, Gerry Manero withdraws $150 from his furniture mart's checking account. Since he is the sole owner of this business, he is now $150 richer, the business has $150 less, and there has been no overall change in Gerry's total cash position. However, the accountant would record only the effect of this transaction on the business. In other words, he would show that the business now has $150 less and would ignore the effect of this transaction on the individual, Gerry. Transactions, therefore, can affect the owner of a business in one way and the business itself in another way.

The business entity principle obviously has limited relevance for the accounting function of the established major corporation. However, many a public accountant has burned the midnight oil in an effort to apply this concept to the combined personal and business records of the individual proprietor.

The Going Concern Principle

Most businesses begin with the basic idea that they will be operated in a logical, rational manner which will lead to success over an extended period of time. This same basic assumption is made by the accountant and is called the "going concern principle." It facilitates the accountant's difficult job of assessing values. To see why this is so, we must discuss the cost concept.

The Cost Concept

Cost, as we all know, doesn't necessarily equal value. Perhaps the most dramatic illustration of this statement is the fact that in the bull market of December 1970, various investors were willing to pay $320 for a share of equity in IBM Corporation when the value of its assets was only $52 per share. The cost concept has its problems and limitations, but no one in the accounting profession has yet been able to come up with an acceptable alternative that provides the same practicality and objectivity.

We saw in Chapter 1 that the listing of assets is a key step in preparing a Balance Sheet. Certainly, it is one of the most basic functions of the accountant. The foundation on which the value of these assets is to be established is obviously a key question. The answer is not as clear-cut as it might appear.

To illustrate, let's again use an example of home ownership. Suppose one morning a prospective buyer looks at your home and asks you what you consider to be its value. Later on in the day, a tax assessor comes to look at your home and asks the same question. Most of us would give one answer to the prospective buyer and another to the tax assessor, whether or not we are honest enough to admit it. The point is that the assessment of value can be a highly subjective process. Herein lies the dilemma. The accountant must bring objectivity to the valuation of a business. For this reason the problem of how to value the assets of a business is an important as well as a nettlesome question. There are several possibilities.

1. Value the assets at their market value. Simple enough—just state the worth of the property today. But this isn't always as easy as it sounds. The value of something can be highly dependent upon the prospective purchaser's particular needs; for this reason, it's possible to get three, four, or five dif-

fering evaluations of the worth of any particular property. The economists call this the theory of "utility." However, if the accountant were to use this concept, he would again run directly into the problem of subjectivity.

2. Value the assets on the basis of the amount of money that would be required to replace them. This replacement value does away with a value range that depends on the prospective buyer's needs. However, the cost of replacing something often depends on how it is replaced. For example, it's standard practice in most businesses to obtain at least three or four bids before major construction is undertaken. The reason, of course, is that the cost can vary depending on who does the work, what material they use, how efficiently they go about the construction, and other factors. The use of a replacement approach will almost surely provide a range rather than a single common value to place on the asset.

3. Determine the value of any particular asset on the basis of its original cost. The advantage in this particular approach, of course, is that it's easy to determine and subsequently document exactly what you paid for something. For example, how would you get a variety of opinions about the value of your attaché case? Some opinions may be based on its so-called market value, or possibly on its replacement value. However, the one cost that you and others could agree on would be the cost you originally incurred to buy it. To establish this cost, you need only to produce the original invoice. This does not necessarily suggest that everyone would agree that you had made a good buy. The fact

remains that you can, on the basis of the original
cost, objectively establish the value of the case. This
is the so-called cost concept.

The objective approach is extremely important to the
accountant, and its practical advantages are obvious. The
cost concept gives the accountant a simple, workable
method by which he can always record asset values on a
Balance Sheet. Executives and businessmen who understand this concept will always know immediately the basis
for the asset values that appear in any Balance Sheet,
since under the cost concept they are always recorded at
original cost.

The primary appeal of the cost concept is its expediency and objectivity. As noted earlier, however, the
going concern concept is also relevant to the question of
determining asset values. Under that principle, the
accountant assumes that there will be little likelihood of
the need to determine asset values in liquidation. Because
it is assumed that the assets will be used in the normal
conduct of the business rather than sold or disposed of,
the question of the value of the assets does not become as
critical as it might otherwise. In this way the going concern principle facilitates the accounting problem of determining the values of assets.

The Realization Principle

A routine business transaction often involves more
steps than meet the eye. Let's take, for example, a ficti-
tious company—EZI Manufacturing Company—and its
sale of widgets. In December, the widgets were manufactured at the factory. In January, the widgets were shipped

This table shows that the application of the realization principle may result in situations where the net income of the business can be affected without a corresponding effect on cash.

The realization principle is the last of the basic ideas that form part of our conceptual groundwork. Clearly, accounting principles—unlike mathematical or scientific principles—are by no means scientifically derived. They are man-made agreements that have evolved over the years as practical aids to solving accounting problems. However, although the use of these accounting principles provides a common and accepted approach to problems associated with the measurement of financial results of a business, there are still an incredible number of ways in which financial results can be presented. Accounting's efforts to cope with this problem are discussed in the next chapter.

4

Accounting
Conventions

T HERE is an old story about a successful applicant for
the job of chief accountant. After many others had failed
to obtain the position, he was hired because he answered
the president's question, "How much is two and two?" by
replying, "How much do you want it to be, Sir?"

Businesses also account for their results in a variety of
ways. For example, almost all companies can obtain discounts for prompt payment. One firm may take these
discounts and reduce the cost of merchandise; another
may take discounts and record them as revenue or income
realized on prompt payments. One firm may build a large
capital facility and consider the associated costs of its own
engineering staff and related corporate efforts as part of
the cost of the facility. Or it may even include in this figure
the first four or five months of operation, classifying them
as start-up costs. A competitive firm, building a similar
facility, may ignore these costs and assume that they are

expenses chargeable against income for revenues during the period in which they were incurred.

These are but a few of numerous ways in which accounting information can be recorded. What is important to recognize is that exactly the same financial information can be presented many ways, all of them in accordance with the principles we have been discussing. Accounting makes an effort to overcome this deficiency through the use of three so-called accepted, basic accounting conventions: consistency, conservatism, and materiality.

The Convention of Consistency

As its name suggests, the convention of consistency says that once a business transaction is accounted for in one particular manner, it must be accounted for in this same way consistently thereafter.

If, for example, a company accounts for cash discounts as revenue or income derived from prompt payments, it must continue to do so in all its succeeding statements of income. This doctrine makes it very difficult for a business to manipulate its figures by showing them on one occasion in a manner that sheds a favorable light on the result and then, when it is convenient, changing to another approach. The convention of consistency is the basis for that portion of the annual audit report of every major publicly held American corporation, which reads to the effect, "This statement has been prepared in accordance with generally accepted accounting principles, on a basis *consistent* with the preceding year."

In a more general sense, Emerson once said, "A foolish consistency is the hobgoblin of little minds." In accounting, however, consistency is designed to prevent the manipulation of accounting data from one accounting period to another. This particular convention facilitates the understanding of accounting data, because once a person understands how a particular business transaction is treated in one particular accounting period, he can expect it to be treated the same way in subsequent periods.

The Convention of Conservatism

Contrary to what might be expected, the convention of conservatism has nothing to do with how people in the accounting profession dress or behave. We have already discussed the inherently objective and conservative nature of the cost and realization concepts. The convention of conservatism is merely an amplification of the same basic approach. It says that whenever the accountant is given the option to do so, he will always choose to reflect financial data in terms of the lower of two possible values.

Perhaps the best example of this occurs in the evaluation of inventories; that is, merchandise held by the company for sale. At the close of the accounting period, the accountant, as we know from the cost concept, would value this inventory on the basis of its cost to the business. If, however, its market value at this point were now lower than its original cost, the accountant would, in accordance with the convention of conservatism, reflect the lower value. Accounting statements, without exception, employ this approach in the evaluation of inventories, and it is sometimes called "the cost or lower-than-market method of evaluation." We can see that it grows out of the convention of conservatism.

Another way in which conservatism is commonly

applied in accounting practice concerns gains and losses from the sale of property. In this situation, "sound" accounting will invariably recognize any loss that has occurred or could possibly occur. On the other hand, "sound" accounting will never recognize profit on the sale of assets until the sale actually takes place.

The major objective of the convention of conservatism, like that of consistency, is to protect the shareholders or owners of a business from a fraudulent or misleading representation of the worth of the business.

The Convention of Materiality

Even though the popular song suggests that "little things mean a lot," they don't to the accountant. This is the essence of the convention of materiality, which says that accounting should not be concerned with immaterial events in the life of a business. But what is "material"? To some of us as individuals, a sum of $2,000 or $3,000 may be quite important and most material, but to any of the corporations in *Fortune* 500 it is rather insignificant.

The convention of materiality, then, really serves as a philosophical basis for expediency. It says that when a particular transaction is not material to the financial results of the business, the accountant can use his own discretion as to when and perhaps how to record that event. The application of the convention of materiality simplifies both the work of the accountant and the structure of his accounting records.

For example, consider the consumption of supplies in the business. Theoretically, each time a piece of paper, a typewriter ribbon, or a pencil is used, it becomes an expense. As a practical matter, nothing could be more ridiculous (or costly, for that matter) than to account for the expenses of a business with this degree of precision. Obviously, twenty pieces of paper aren't material to the business. Common sense, as well as the convention of materiality, allows the accountant a much more expedient approach. He takes only the total costs for the month or even an average of several months' costs of supplies as the expense.

The convention of materiality lies behind the frequent rhetoric in published financial statements, which often read, "In the opinion of legal counsel there are no contingencies of material significance," or similar phrasing. Although the convention of materiality serves a highly useful purpose in simplifying the work of the accountant, the user of financial information must be constantly aware that its application is always left to the judgment of the individual accountant. Therefore, when the convention is called into play, the practicing nonfinancial executive should make sure that what is material or immaterial to the accountant is also material or immaterial to the management and shareholders of a business.

In these last two chapters we have covered the fundamental principles and conventions that in combination make up the so-called structural framework of accounting. With this groundwork laid, let us now look in greater depth and detail at the two basic accounting statements, the Balance Sheet and the Income Statement.

5

Financial Photography:
Balance Sheets and
Income Statements

WE can think of a business, whether it is a simple proprietorship or a large corporation, as a continuum of business events over a period of time. There are two kinds of events in this continuum. First, there are transactions which change only the status and balance of assets or liabilities. These involve the exchange of one asset for another or an increase in liabilities in exchange for assets. They only affect accounts on a Balance Sheet and are Balance Sheet transactions. Second, there are transactions which affect the status of assets, liabilities, and also revenue and expense accounts. They are Income Statement transactions.

Although neither profession may welcome the comparison, it is useful to draw a parallel between the work of the accountant and that of the photographer. Both record events, the photographer with his camera and the accountant with his ledger. We can take the analogy further by thinking of the Balance Sheet and Income Statement as forms of photography, albeit financial photography. Exhibit 2 presents this analogy graphically.

In Chapter 1, we looked at the dual aspect concept and its importance to the *theory* of the Balance Sheet. In developing this concept, we followed on a day-in, day-out basis the events relating to the hypothetical business venture of Gerry Manero. As we developed this illustration we saw that a Balance Sheet reported the status of a business's assets and liabilities, which were constantly changing. Each day the various items on the Balance Sheet changed according to that particular day's transactions, and the Balance Sheet reflected the status of a business's assets and liabilities at only one given moment. For this reason, the Balance Sheet was always dated.

The similarity between a Balance Sheet and a photographic snapshot is clear. A snapshot captures a situation only at the given moment in time when the picture is taken. Many actions precede the snapshot and others follow it, but the permanent image is the one that remains at the precise moment the still shot was snapped. In exactly the same way, many business actions take place before and after the Balance Sheet is drawn up. The Balance Sheet in the fancy annual report of a major corporation is something more of a formal portrait, but it remains a still life—a static report on the business at a particular moment.

The Income Statement, which we discussed in Chapter 2, is similar to another type of photography. The Income Statement is a mechanism which accumulates the effect of each day's transactions. In the case of Gerry Manero's business, the Income Statement accumulated the sales for

Exhibit 2. Financial photograph: balance sheet and income statement transactions.

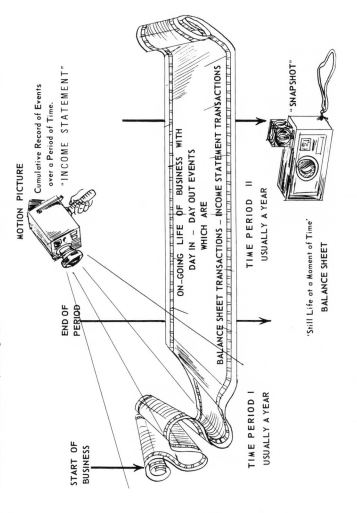

MOTION PICTURE

Cumulative Record of Events over a Period of Time.

"INCOME STATEMENT"

ON-GOING LIFE OF BUSINESS WITH DAY IN – DAY OUT EVENTS WHICH ARE

BALANCE SHEET TRANSACTIONS – INCOME STATEMENT TRANSACTIONS

END OF PERIOD

START OF BUSINESS

TIME PERIOD I
USUALLY A YEAR

TIME PERIOD II
USUALLY A YEAR

"SNAPSHOT"

'Still Life at a Moment of Time'
BALANCE SHEET

one day, then another, and so on, so that the total sales transacted up to the date the Income Statement was prepared were reflected in that statement. Thus an Income Statement captures and amasses in one record everything that goes on in a business over a period of time. In photography, the form which captures all action and events as they occur and makes a permanent record of them is, of course, the motion picture. In like manner, the Income Statement permanently records the business actions as they occur during the period in which they are being "photographed" by the accountant.

Our analogy to photography demonstrates some of the basic differences between the Income Statement and the Balance Sheet. At the same time, however, it is important to clearly understand the close relationship between them. Let's look again at the Balance Sheets and Income Statements we prepared for Gerry Manero. These are given in Exhibit 3, which shows that the increase in owner's equity between July 27 and September 15 is exactly the same amount that is shown as the net income on the Income Statement for the same period.

If Gerry had taken $200 of the net income and the business before preparing the Balance Sheet on September 15, 1971, this amount would have had to be reflected in the Balance Sheet and would have modified the owner's equity section of the Balance Sheet in this way:

Owner's equity	$600
Less drawings	200
Net owner's equity	$400

Under these circumstances, the increase in owner's equity from one Balance Sheet to another would be equal

Exhibit 3. Relationship between balance sheets and income statement for Manero's Furniture Mart.

BALANCE SHEET
July 27, 1971

Cash	*Owner's Equity*
$15,000	$15,000

BALANCE SHEET
September 15, 1971

Assets		*Liabilities and Owner's Equity*	
Cash	$10,600	Accounts payable	$ 2,000
Accounts receivable	800	Loans payable	5,000
Inventory	6,200	Total liabilities	$ 7,000
Delivery truck	5,000	Owner's equity	15,600
Total	$22,600	Total	$22,600

OWNER'S EQUITY

July 27	*September 15*	*Increase*
$15,000	$15,600	$600

INCOME STATEMENT
September 15, 1971

Revenues	$2,400
Less cost of goods sold	1,800
Net increase	$ 600

Exhibit 4. Relationship between balance sheet and income statement, General Motors (millions of dollars).

BALANCE SHEET
December 31

Assets	1970	1971	Liabilities, Reserves, and Stockholders' Equity	1970	1971
Current assets	$ 6,234	$ 7,698	Current liabilities	$ 3,244	$ 3,346
Investments and miscellaneous assets	1,085	1,185	Other liabilities	420	831
Real estate, plants, and equipment	6,396	5,655	Reserves	395	415
Other assets	342	282	Stockholders' equity	9,998	10,228
Totals	$14,057	$14,820	Totals	$14,057	$14,820

OWNER'S (SHAREHOLDERS') EQUITY

1970	1971	Increase
$9,998	$10,228	$230

INCOME STATEMENT
For Year End December 31, 1971

Revenues		$18,880
Less		
Cost of sales	$15,596	
Other expenses	2,675	
Total		$18,271
Net income for year		$ 609
Less distributed to owners as dividends		$379
Increase in owner's (shareholders') equity		$230

to the net income for the period less any net income drawn by Gerry Manero.

Exhibit 4 shows a comparison between a set of Balance Sheets and an Income Statement for General Motors. The reader will note the same link between the increase in owner's (in this case, shareholders') equity from one Balance Sheet to another and the net income for the period as per the Income Statement.

The Balance Sheet

With some of these general ideas in mind, let's turn to a more detailed examination of the basic structure and terminology of the Balance Sheet and Income Statement. The Balance Sheets we have prepared for Gerry Manero have been purposely brief and simple. For a larger, more complex business, they would need to be expanded.

Also, the shareholders and managers of a business are often interested in a greater amount of detail. Over a period of time, a standard Balance Sheet format for the presentation of a business's basic financial data has evolved, in which assets are subdivided into three major categories: current assets, fixed assets, and other assets.

Current Assets

The four items described below are the most common forms of current assets, although there could be others. Assets are classified as current as long as they are cash, or can be converted into cash, within the customary operating period of the business (usually one year). Current assets, therefore, are cash or assets which can become the equivalent of cash within one year's time.

Cash. Cash usually represents the funds on hand held by the business, that is, bills or coin and funds that are readily available in checking accounts. It would not include cash funds for which there was some legal constraint against using, such as funds held in special deposits or in escrow.

Marketable Securities. Marketable securities represent temporary investments in the stocks or bonds in other businesses or enterprises, and possibly governmental bonds. Next to cash, they are usually the most liquid assets, and can be turned into cash on short notice.

Accounts Receivable. Accounts receivable represent monies owed to the firm by customers for the purchase of merchandise. Accounts receivable are created when goods or services are provided and the business receives a legally enforceable promise of payment rather than cash. In our personal lives, we create accounts receivable whenever we buy merchandise on credit and then wait to make payment on it until we receive a statement of account for the purchase. Accounts receivable are often shown as a gross amount of accounts receivable, and then a "reserve for doubtful accounts" is shown as a deduction. This reserve represents an estimate of accounts receivable on which the business does not expect to be able to collect. (We will discuss the accounting of doubtful accounts receivable in more detail in subsequent chapters.)

Inventories. Inventories represent merchandise which has been purchased by a business and is being held in stock until such time as it is resold. Gerry Manero's Furniture Mart is an example of this type of inventory. When a business manufactures its own product for sale, inventories include the value of the merchandise or product that has been manufactured and is being held in readiness for sale. Moreover, such a business often needs raw materials from which to make the product. Also, at any given time certain products are invariably in the process of being manufactured. Both of these inventories are made in addition to the finished products inventory. Many manufacturing companies often show their inventories in this order: raw material inventories, goods in process inventories, and finished goods inventories.

Prepaid Expenses. Prepaid expenses are those which have been paid in advance by the business. They constitute a right to a future service which will be used, but has not yet been used, by the business. This is what gives them their value. A common example of a prepaid expense is the insurance coverage a business pays for in advance of receiving services.

Fixed Assets

Fixed assets consist of tangible permanent investments in so-called capital facilities, usually brick and mortar, or equipment. In many Balance Sheets, these particular assets are much more descriptively and accurately labeled "property," "plant," and "equipment."

Almost all these fixed assets are shown in the following order in the Balance Sheet: gross fixed assets, reserve for accumulated depreciation, and net fixed assets.

The term "gross fixed assets" refers to the original value; that is, the cost which was incurred to purchase or construct the physical facility (note the application of the cost concept). Gross fixed assets are reduced by an item called reserve for accumulated depreciation. Depreciation is a major accounting concept in itself, which we shall discuss in detail in subsequent chapters. At this point, let us define depreciation as an estimate of how much the original value of all the company's assets have decreased owing to usage, passage of time, obsolescence, or a combination of these. This amount is deducted from the gross fixed assets to arrive at the figure for net fixed assets, which is the value (that is, the cost) of the fixed assets diminished by the depreciation that has accumulated to the date of the financial statement.

Other Assets

Other assets, the third and final classification of assets on the Balance Sheet, include various assets which cannot readily be classified as either current or fixed. Other assets, like fixed assets, tend to be long term. The most common of these is investments. A company can have marketable securities which are also investments. Investments shown under this heading of other assets usually differ in several respects from marketable securities. First, they are intended to be held for an extended period of time—at least one year or longer. Second, they are being held to control the company owned or to earn a significant return on the holding, or both.

Intangible Assets. Intangible assets are another common form of other assets. They include patents, copyrights, franchises, and similar matters. These assets can have a significant value in generating income for the business, but they are distinct in their form from the tangibility of, say, a plant.

Liabilities and Shareholders' Equities. The right-hand side of the Balance Sheet consists of the claims on the assets of a corporation. These are: (1) liabilities, which are the claims of the creditors, and (2) the claims of the owners, which are owner's equities. The liabilities and owner's equities sections of a Balance Sheet are also broken down to standard subclassifications: current liabilities, long-term liabilities, and shareholders' equity.

Current Liabilities

Current liabilities include obligations which are expected to fall due within the next accounting period (usually the next year). This particular definition corresponds to the same time parameter used in the definition of current assets. The most common types of current liabilities are described below.

Accounts Payable. Accounts payable represent the counterpart of accounts receivable. With an account payable, the business is a debtor rather than a creditor. Thus, it has a legal obligation to make a payment rather than to receive it.

Notes Payable. Notes payable are similar to accounts payable. Usually the legal instrument associated with this obligation is much more formal and will involve a longer period of time for payment. A note payable, like an account payable, has its converse in the note receivable, which is shown on the left-hand side of the Balance Sheet as an asset.

Accrued Liabilities. Under law, the term "accrue" means to become a present right or enforceable demand. In accounting, the term is used similarly, and accrued liabilities represent obligations of the business which have not yet been paid. Such obligations can take several forms and may or may not be indicated separately on the Balance Sheet. One of the most common to be shown separately is accrued taxes, which could include federal, state, or local income taxes as well as real estate taxes.

Another customary type of accrued liability is wages

and salaries owed to workers and employees for services they have already provided to the business.

Long-Term Liabilities

Long-term liabilities include those debts (or claims on assets) which fall due a year or longer in the future. Long-term liabilities are usually incurred to obtain more permanent funds for the business. They are often shown according to the source of funds, as described below.

Bank Loans. Funds obtained from bank loans can be either a short- or long-term liability. If they are due and payable within one year from the date of the Balance Sheet, they are classified as a short-term liability. If they are payable in more than a year, they are classified as a long-term liability and would be shown in this section of the Balance Sheet.

Bonds. These are another form of long-term capital. Bonds are also loans that are often obtained from many people who are given certificates, called "bonds," as evidence of a loan. Bonds usually have extended 15- to 20-year repayment periods.

Shareholders' Equity

The lower left-hand section of the Balance Sheet contains the shareholders' (or owner's) equity section. Shareholders' equities, as we have discussed, represent the claim the owners have on the assets of the business after the obligations to all other creditors have been fulfilled. There are usually two basic forms of shareholders' equity, as described below.

Common Stock. Common stock (or capital stock) represents the original contribution to the business that has been made by the owners. In the case of an individual proprietorship, such as that of Gerry Manero, this contribution represents the original amount of the funds he has put into the business. In the case of a corporation, the contribution may be a large number of shares which have been sold to thousands of individual investors through an established public stock exchange. Under any form of business structure, these are the funds originally contributed by the owners of the business. They are to be used to purchase assets and conduct the affairs subsequent to formation of the business.

Retained Earnings. Retained earnings is the second classification under shareholders' equity. The retained earnings of the business represent the total cumulative net income that a business earns over its life, less any funds which have been returned to the owners in the form of dividends. We showed the buildup of retained earnings for a period of one year for both Gerry Manero and General Motors in Exhibits 3 and 4.

In the past, the term "earned surplus" was frequently used to describe the retained earnings of a business. In some instances, this phrase is still used. However, it is appropriately falling into disuse, since "surplus" is misleading. The funds are not surplus because they have been ploughed back into the business to provide monies for expansion and growth.

The Income Statement

In the early stages of the development of American industry, assets tended to be the determining factor in the worth of a business. For this reason, investors' and shareholders' attention focused primarily on a company's

Balance Sheet. Times have changed, however, and the American investor now emphasizes the so-called growth potential of the corporation. Generally, this is the ability of a corporation to sustain a constantly increasing rate of growth in net income year after year.

This change has switched attention from the Balance Sheet to the Income Statement. Let's look at a typical Income Statement, as shown in Exhibit 5.

Sales

The first item on this Income Statement is "sales." Sometimes this item is called "sales revenue" or just "revenue," but, whatever its title, it refers to the amounts received (or to be received—accounts receivable) for goods or services provided (or, under the realization principle, delivered) to other organizations in the conduct of its business for the period shown, in our example, during 1971.

Exhibit 5. A typical income statement for the year ended 1971.

Sales	$3,100,000
Less cost of goods sold	2,350,000
Gross profit	$ 750,000
Less operating expenses	
Selling expenses	250,000
Administrative expenses	200,000
Operating profit	$ 300,000
Provision for income taxes	144,000
Net income	$ 156,000

Cost of Goods Sold

The second item on the Income Statement is "cost of goods sold." As in our illustration, it is usually shown as "less cost of goods sold" since it is deducted from "sales." The term had the same meaning when we used it to prepare Gerry Manero's Income Statement. It represents what it cost the business to either purchase or manufacture the goods they have sold in order to generate the revenues that appear in the first line, "sales." In most businesses, other than those providing a service, cost of goods sold represents the most significant item of expense for the business. For this reason, it is almost always shown as a separate item.

Gross Profit

The subtraction of "cost of goods sold" from "sales" leaves a remainder called "gross profit," the third item on the Income Statement. Gross profit is almost invariably shown as a separate item on an Income Statement. It indicates the income that remains to cover the expenses of selling the product and administering the business.

These two expenses are shown next on an Income Statement as "operating expenses," which are the expenses incurred to operate the business for the period of the Income Statement. Sometimes they are shown as a single item or subdivided, as in our illustration, into the two major components, "selling expenses" and "administrative expenses." Selling expenses include the cost of sales organization, sales promotions, and similar factors. Administrative expenses cover the cost of managing the organization and typically include insurance costs, rent, heat, light, accounting, legal costs, and so on.

Operating Profit

Operating expenses reduce the amount of the company's gross profit and must be covered before net income can be generated. The deduction of operating expenses from gross profit leaves the business's "operating profit," which is shown as another separate subtotal and represents profit that has been provided from the normal operations of the business. Many Income Statements make a distinction between operating and nonoperating profits in order to differentiate the net income generated as a result of the normal routine conduct of the business from the net income generated by sale of equipment or property or some other, similar transaction not normally considered the basic function of the business. Sometimes operating profit is described as "net income before taxes."

Income Taxes

The next item on the Income Statement is "provision for income taxes." Income taxes, which have become a significant item for reducing business income, are almost always shown separately.

Net Income

The final line on the Income Statement, "net income," is, of course, the most critical piece of information, the final net result of operating the business for the period covered by the Income Statement. Net income, as we have stressed before, represents the increment (or if there is a net loss, the decrement) that has resulted from successful operation of the business for the period of time covered by the Income Statement.

Balance Sheets and Income Statements are the output of accounting systems. We turn next to a more detailed discussion of certain special accounting problems and concepts involved in obtaining this output.

6

Special Accounting Problems

In this chapter, we'll look at three special accounting problems: (1) fixed assets accounting, which includes depreciation costs; (2) inventory accounting, which is the cost of goods sold determination; and (3) accounts receivable, which is accounting for bad debts.

These three areas are given special attention for two reasons. First, they involve some concepts, procedures, and terminology which are critical to the proper understanding and utilization of financial data. Second, they include areas which the nonfinancial executive often finds troublesome and difficult to understand.

Fixed Assets

In Chapter 4, we defined fixed assets as permanent investments of a long-term nature in so-called capital facilities. These include property, plant, and equipment that will be used by the business to provide goods or services.

Recording Original Value

The first logical question concerning fixed asset accounting is: On what basis should their value be recorded? The application of the cost principle gives the answer to this question—which is cost.

The next question then becomes: Exactly what makes up the cost? The answer has become well defined in accounting practice and can be summarized as follows:

1. The cost of fixed assets includes all costs of obtaining and installing the fixed assets. For example, assume that a business purchases a piece of land for $5,000. There is a $250 payment to the real estate agent along with a $500 fee to the lawyer for the closing. Finally, there is a cost of $1,000 for clearing and filling the property. In this instance, the cost of the fixed asset includes all these costs because they were required to make the facility ready for use by the business.

    Another example could be the purchase of a piece of machinery, with the cost of transportation and installation included in the fixed cost. Thus the basic cost of the machinery might be $1,000, but there is an additional $200 installation cost and a $100 freight charge. Then the total cost of the fixed asset is recorded on the books as $1,300.

2. A business may construct a machine or a building, using its own labor, or some of its own labor, for the partial construction or installation. The costs

the company incurs for this labor are included as part of the asset.
3. A business may acquire a new asset, the payment of which is made partly in cash and partly in the value of the old assets traded in. For example, if a business pays $500 cash for a calculating machine which has a trade-in value of $300, the total real cost of the new calculating machine is $800, not $500, and $800 is the figure used to record the total cost of the asset.

Depreciation

We have said that fixed assets include property, plant, and equipment that will be used by the business to provide goods or services. The buildings, equipment, and machinery used for this purpose day after day will obviously wear out and ultimately become useless. As this process takes place, the original value of the asset decreases, with a corresponding reduction in the owner's equity. To illustrate this process, let's trace an example in a series of simplified Balance Sheets.

Event. A delivery service is started with a $5,000 purchase of delivery truck by the owner.

Balance Sheet
Delivery Service
Beginning of Year

Assets		*Equities*	
Fixed assets	$5,000	Owner's equity	$5,000

Event. Delivery service is operated for a year, but the truck now has less value, since it is older and has been used. The truck now has a value of only $3,500.

Balance Sheet
Delivery Service
End of Year

Assets		*Equity*	
Fixed assets	$3,500	Owner's equity	$3,500

In this example, reduction in the asset value has been taken as a direct deduction to owner's equity. We know, however, that under regular procedures this would be done by reflecting the amount as an expense (which is also a reduction of owner's equity) in an Income Statement. The process of taking the estimated usage of an asset each year and charging it as an expense against the business is called "depreciation."

The more technologically oriented a business is, the more important the factor of obsolescence becomes, although depreciation includes the effect of both factors. We should clarify, however, that not all fixed assets are depreciated. Fixed assets include land as well as plant and equipment. The value of land tends to be permanent. When it is used as a building site (other than being mined or farmed), it does not wear out. In fact, it tends to appreciate in value. For these reasons the accountant does not depreciate land.

Other types of fixed assets do wear out, and to calculate the expense associated with this process of depreciation, the accountant has to determine three facts:

1. The original cost of the asset, which is usually determined in accordance with the principles set forth at the outset of this chapter.
2. The estimated life of the asset.
3. The estimated residual or scrap value, if any, of the asset at the end of its life.

Let's apply these three factors to determine the depreciation of a fixed asset, remembering that our objective is to determine the estimated usage of the asset and to record it as an expense during the period when it is used to produce revenues for the business.

Assume that a business purchases a machine with a basic factory cost of $1,000, and there are also $100 of costs to deliver it and another $100 to install it on the premises. Applying the guidelines we have just discussed, we can readily determine that the total original cost of the fixed asset would be $1,200.

The next step is to determine the estimated salvage value. Almost all machinery has some residual value—when it is disposed of. The word "estimated" here is critical because, of course, this can be nothing more than an educated guess as to what the machine will be worth at the time of disposal. Although this is a difficult guess to make, it is by no means impossible. Let's assume that on the basis of past experience and/or consultation with used-machinery dealers, the accountant concludes that the final estimated salvage value of the machinery would be $200. Now that we have the original cost of the fixed asset as well as the estimated salvage value, we can determine the estimated net cost of the asset, which is simply the difference between these two—in our case, $1,000.

The next step is to determine the estimated use for life. There are a variety of sources from which the accountant can obtain the estimated useful life. One of the most common is the guidelines issued by the Internal Revenue Service. Others are engineering, equipment, manpower, and other associations. Assume that we arrive at an estimate of four years. We now have all three elements we need to arrive at our estimated annual depreciation

expense, which we can calculate to be $250 per year. This
is obtained by dividing the estimated net cost of the fixed
asset, that is, the original $1,200 of cost less the estimated
salvage value of $200, by the useful life period of four
years, as shown below:

Purchase price of asset	$1,000
Delivery cost	100
Installation cost	100
Total cost of asset	$1,200
Less estimated salvage value	200
Asset cost to be depreciated	$1,000

$$\frac{\$1,000 \text{ (asset cost to be depreciated)}}{4 \text{ years}} = \$250 \text{ per year}$$

If we were to plot this process graphically, it would
appear as shown in Exhibit 6.

Exhibit 6. Straight-line depreciation.

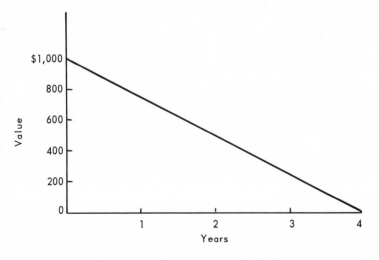

Thus, the process of depreciating the estimated net cost of the fixed asset in equal annual amounts of depreciation expense results in a straight line. Therefore, this technique for determining depreciation expense is called "the straight-line method of depreciation." It is simple in both conception and application, and is the most commonly used approach in American business. Applying this method, the resulting usage cost or depreciation expense becomes the same for each year of the estimated useful life of the asset.

In real life, however, assets do not always necessarily wear out or obsolesce at the same rate each year. The straight-line method of depreciation ignores this fact. As an everyday example of this phenomenon, consider your own automobile, on which the obsolescence factor is much more pronounced in the earlier years of ownership and operation. The same holds true in many business situations.

For this reason, two different so-called accelerated methods of depreciation have been developed during the last fifteen years and have become accepted accounting practice. Unlike the straight-line method, which takes equal annual amounts for usage, accelerated methods take more of the expense for the usage of the asset at the beginning of its life than at the end. There are two accelerated methods of depreciation, which are described below.

Sum of the Years Digits. The formula for calculating sum-of-the-years-digits depreciation is a fraction, with the numerator representing the years of remaining useful life of the asset and the denominator indicating the sum of the digits of the years of estimated useful life. Using this approach, we would depreciate the machine with a net asset value of $1,000 in the following way:

Step 1. Calculate the sum of the digits of the years of

estimated useful life; that is, 4 years = 1 + 2 + 3 + 4 = 10.

Step 2. Determine depreciation to be taken in each year, starting in the first year, for the number of years of remaining useful life.

Year of Life	Years Remaining	Rate Fraction		Percent
1	4	⁴⁄₁₀	=	40
2	3	³⁄₁₀	=	30
3	2	²⁄₁₀	=	20
4	1	¹⁄₁₀	=	10
10	10			100

Double Declining Balance. The first step in the double-declining-balance method is to determine the rate of depreciation by means of the straight-line method. This figure is then doubled, and then always taken on the declining balance of the value of the asset. The following steps illustrate the double-declining-balance method, again using the machine with a net asset value of $1,000 as an example.

Step 1. Determine rate of depreciation under straight-line method; that is, four years or 25%.

Step 2. Double rate of depreciation used under straight-line method; that is, 25% × 2 = 50%.

Step 3. Apply rate, always using the declining balance of net asset as the value.

Year	Value	Rate, %	Depreciation	Declining Value
1	$1,000.00	50	$500.00	$500.00
2	500.00	50	250.00	250.00
3	250.00	50	125.00	125.00
4	125.00	50	62.50	62.50
5	62.50	50	31.25	31.25
6	31.25	50	15.62	15.62

Reserves for Accumulated Depreciation

In accounting, the assets of a business are subject to an invariable life cycle. As they are used to generate revenues for the business, they become an expense. Thus, cash may be used to pay a salesman who is generating revenue through his selling efforts. The asset of cash decreases, and the expense of selling increases.

Merchandise inventory is an asset. When the merchandise is sold, the asset inventory decreases, and the expense of cost of goods sold increases.

The prepayment of insurance premiums results in an asset, prepaid expenses. However, as this insurance coverage is utilized with the passage of time, the asset of prepaid insurance decreases, and the expense of insurance increases.

In accounting for fixed assets, we follow this same approach. Since the fixed asset is consumed in the life of the business, the cost of its usage is taken as an expense called depreciation. The time period involved is longer, and estimates must be made, but the basic procedure, as in all other cases, is to decrease the asset as it is used and increase the expense.

There is one additional difference: The value of the fixed asset on the Balance Sheet is not reduced directly, as was the case with other forms of assets. Instead, the accountant accumulates these reductions in a special account so that they can be shown separately on the Balance Sheet. This special account is called a reserve for accumulated depreciation. As depreciation expense is incurred, the accountant increases this cumulative account (sometimes called a "contra account") and at the same time increases the item of depreciation expense that appears in the Income Statement.

The purpose behind this process is to allow fixed assets to always appear on the Balance Sheet at their original gross value. The extent to which they have been used can then be determined from the accumulated depreciation account in order to arrive at the estimated net fixed value of the assets. This procedure provides more information to the reader of the financial statement. Fixed assets stay on the Balance Sheet even though they may be 100 percent depreciated. Thus, it is possible for fixed assets to appear on a Balance Sheet in the following manner:

Fixed Assets

Gross (property, plant, and equipment)	$283,000
Less reserve for accumulated depreciation	282,000
	$ 1,000

At the time a fixed asset is actually disposed of, the gain or loss on its sale is shown as a nonoperating profit or loss in the Income Statement. If the fixed asset is sold at an amount greater than originally estimated as its salvage value, there is a gain. If it is sold at an amount less, there is a loss.

Inventory Accounting

Let us turn now to the second special problem area, inventory accounting, which is concerned with the asset item of inventories and the expense factor of cost of goods sold. Earlier we defined the cost of goods sold as the cost of the product purchased for resale and/or manufactured which is ultimately sold to obtain revenue. The cost of goods sold, except in the case of service industries, is by far the largest element of cost in an Income Statement and is therefore one of the most important items of expense. Since the accountant must always try to match expenses with revenues, only the costs of the goods which have been sold to generate sales revenue will be included in the cost of the goods sold for the period.

Perpetual Inventory Accounting Procedures

In some businesses the process of determining the cost of goods sold is relatively easy. Take, for example, a yacht dealer. Because he has very few sales, his inventory accounting problems are simple. He has little trouble keeping track of what he buys and sells. When he purchases a yacht for cash, he exchanges one asset (cash) for another (inventory). When the yacht is sold again for cash, these things happen: (1) his asset of cash increases, (2) his revenue increases at the same time, (3) his asset of inventory decreases, and (4) his expense of cost of goods sold increases. Thus, if the yacht in question cost $10,000 and was sold for $12,000, the net result would be net income of $2,000.

When a business has a limited number of sales, but of a high value, such as yachts, the accountant can easily and practically maintain a record of each individual item in inventory and easily determine the value of inventories and the cost of goods sold. This approach is called "perpetual inventory accounting," and although it's simple, it's practical only for low-volume, high-price businesses where each sale represents a significant part of revenue.

Deductive Inventory Accounting Procedures

By way of contrast, think of a common dime store or supermarket where for twelve hours a day literally thousands of transactions take place. Cash registers ring constantly as customers check out and leave the store with merchandise. The perpetual inventory accounting practices that are used for the yacht dealer are impossible in this situation. The cost of goods sold must be deduced. This can easily be done as long as the following information is available: goods on hand at the beginning of a period, goods purchased during the period, and goods on hand at the end of the period.

Information concerning the goods on hand at the beginning and end of the period can be obtained simply by taking a physical count of the merchandise and valuing it on the basis of the price at which it was purchased. The value of the goods purchased during the period can be obtained from records maintained for this purpose. As an illustration, assume the records of a dime store show the following:

Goods on hand, March 31, 1971	$10,000
Purchases during April 1971	13,000
Goods on hand, April 30, 1971	7,000

By logical deduction from these facts, we can conclude that the $10,000 of merchandise on hand at the beginning of April, together with the $13,000 purchased during April, left us with total goods available for sale of $23,000 during April. If at the end of April, $7,000 of goods were on hand, then $16,000 worth of goods must have been sold during that month.

A more conventional, formal accounting presentation of these same facts would appear as follows:

Beginning inventory, April 1, 1971	$10,000
Purchases	13,000
Goods available	$23,000
Less closing inventory	7,000
Cost of goods sold	$16,000

We can see that the closing inventory for one period must, of course, be the beginning inventory for the subsequent period. The closing inventory value used in the formula to deduce cost of goods sold is the same one shown as the asset of inventory on the Balance Sheet.

Using this approach, the determination of cost of goods sold involved the use of deductive inventory accounting procedures. These procedures are a practical way to account for the cost of goods sold for businesses which have a high-volume and/or low-value sales pattern. It is important to recognize that in deducing the cost of goods sold, an implicit procedural assumption is made that the merchandise has actually been sold. This may not always be the case, for in fact there may have been shrinkage, spoilage, or even pilferage of the merchandise. The user of accounting data should always bear this possibility in mind when looking at the accountant's cost of goods sold.

Inventory Valuation

Deductive and perpetual inventory accounting procedures provide the accountant with two different methods to use to tally, or register, business inventories and to obtain the cost of goods sold. Additional complexities can be, and often are, associated with the inventory valuation process.

Let's take as an example Gerry Manero's brother, who is the owner of a service station. He, like Gerry, is preparing accounting records for his business. At the end of April he deduced his cost of goods sold in accordance with that date:

Inventories
Regular Motor Gasoline

	No. of Gallons	Price per Gallon	Value
Opening inventory, April 1	10,000	20¢	$2,000
Purchases in April	12,000	20¢	2,400
Goods available	22,000		$4,400
Less ending inventory, April 30	8,000		1,600
Cost of goods sold for April	14,000		$2,800

There is no problem here. However, in the following month the cost he had to pay for gasoline increased 3 cents a gallon. Data for the month of May appeared as shown below:

Inventories
Regular Motor Gasoline

	No. of Gallons	Price per Gallon	Value
Opening inventory, May 1	8,000	20¢	$1,600
Purchases in May	10,000	23¢	2,300
Goods available	18,000		$3,900
Less inventory, May 31	10,000		
Cost of goods sold for May	8,000		

As a result of the price change, we now have a problem finding the value of the closing inventory. By deduction, we know that during the month of May, Gerry's brother sold 8,000 gallons of gasoline. What we don't know is whether they were bought at the new price of 23 cents a gallon, or at the old price of 20 cents a gallon. All the gallons are in the same tank and physically indistinguishable from each other, so the answer is by no means clear-cut. The dilemma is placed squarely in the lap of the accountant. He can resolve this particular problem in one of several ways.

First, he can make a so-called FIFO assumption. FIFO is an acronym for "First In, First Out." FIFO assumes that goods which enter into an inventory first are sold first. If in our particular illustration the accountant were to employ the FIFO assumption, the May valuation of inventories and cost of goods sold for Gerry's brother would appear as follows:

Inventories
Regular Motor Gasoline
FIFO APPROACH

	No. of Gallons	Price per Gallon	Value
Opening inventory, May 1	8,000	20¢	$1,600
Purchases in May	10,000	23¢	2,300
Goods available	18,000		$3,900
Less ending inventory, May 31	10,000	23¢	2,300
Cost of goods sold for May	8,000	20¢	$1,600

We can see that under the FIFO assumption, the most current purchases, that is, those made at 23 cents per gallon, are shown as part of the inventory rather than as the cost of goods sold during the accounting period.

A second alternate approach the accountant can employ is LIFO, which stands for "Last In, First Out." The LIFO approach is exactly the opposite of the FIFO approach. It assumes the most recent purchases are the ones that have been sold. There, the value of the goods shown in inventory is at the older purchase cost. Under LIFO, the inventory calculation in our example would be changed as follows:

Inventory
Regular Motor Gasoline
LIFO Approach

	No. of Gallons	Price per Gallon	Value
Opening inventory, May 1	8,000	20¢	$1,600
Purchases in May	10,000	23¢	2,300
Goods available	18,000		$3,900
Less ending inventory, May 31	10,000*		2,060
Cost of goods sold for May	8,000	23¢	$1,840

*Made up of 2,000 gallons at 23¢ = $460, and 8,000 gallons at 20¢ = $1,600.

A third alternative is the Average Method, under which the accountant simply averages the costs of the opening inventory and purchases and then the cost of the goods sold for the period at this average. Under this approach we would have the following:

Inventory
Regular Motor Gasoline
Average Method

	No. of Gallons	Price per Gallon	Value
Opening inventory, May 1	8,000	20¢	$1,600
Purchases in May	10,000	23¢	2,300
Goods available	18,000		$3,900
Less ending inventory, May 31	10,000*		2,170
Cost of goods sold for May	8,000		$1,730

*Derived: $3,900 ÷ 18,000 gallons = 21.66¢ per gallon rounded off to 21.7¢ per gallon.

It is important to recognize that the accountant's choice of method will have an influence on the financial results for the period. A comparison of the gross profit from the sale of regular gasoline for May under the three inventory valuation methods gives these results:

Regular Motor Gasoline
Gross Profit Comparison

	LIFO	FIFO	Average
Sales: 8,000 gallons @ 30¢	$2,400	$2,400	$2,400
Less cost of goods sold	1,840	1,600	1,730
Gross profit	$ 560	$ 800	$ 670
Inventory value to be shown on balance sheet	$2,060	$2,300	$2,170

Under the LIFO approach, the cost of goods sold is higher than it is under either the FIFO or the Average Method. As a consequence, profits will be lower.

Since the end of World War II, the costs of services and materials in the United States have clearly been increasing. When this happens, the use of LIFO inventory evaluation methods tends to lower net income. Since lower net income results in lower tax payments to the United States government, it has been very much in the interest of business to use the LIFO method of inventory evaluation, and it is the most commonly used method in American business today. The important fact for the nonfinancial executive to appreciate, however, is that the accountant does have options, and that the method he chooses can have a significant influence on the so-called final net book results of the business.

Accounts Receivable

We turn now to the final special accounting problem, which is accounts receivable. Almost all businesses must sell on credit. When they do, they receive an account receivable (a legal obligation to be paid) in lieu of cash. Accounts receivable appear on the Balance Sheet as an asset. If for some reason the account receivable cannot be collected, it has no value. Fortunately, most accounts receivable are collected, and in fact, sound credit practices should prevent a business from selling on credit to anyone from whom it doesn't think it can collect. Despite these precautions, every business ends up with some uncollectable accounts. Various accounting methods are used to deal with this particular aspect of business life.

The most direct approach is simply to write off a bad debt once it becomes clear that payment will not be received. When this is done, the accountant reduces the value of accounts receivable by the amount of the write-off and increases the expense, and the uncollected payment is called a "bad debt." The problem with this approach is that the accountant has to wait for an actual bad debt loss to transpire before it can be recognized. In the interim, however, the asset of accounts receivable is not shown in either the most realistic or the most conservative manner, since it is a known fact that all the accounts receivable won't be collected. What is not known is who won't pay and the amounts. To overcome this problem, the general practice is to make a comprehensive estimate of the total amount of accounts receivable that won't be collected. This estimate is called a "reserve for doubtful accounts receivable." The reserve is taken as a reduction from the accounts receivable on the Balance Sheet and usually appears as shown below:

Accounts receivable	$200,000
Less reserve for doubtful accounts	7,000
	$193,000

At the same time the reserve for doubtful accounts is created and used to decrease the value of the asset, a corresponding increase occurs in the expense—bad debts.

The actual amount that is to be set up as reserve for doubtful accounts is usually based on the firm's past experience. Management may determine that a certain percentage of the annual net sales, say 2 to 3 percent, is appropriate. Alternately, it may make a similar determination on the basis of only its credit sales. When this is done, the reserve is reflected in the Balance Sheet, as was shown above.

On the occasion of an actual bad debt write-off, both the asset of accounts receivable and the reserve are reduced by the amount of the write-off. If we assume a write-off of $1,000, the figures shown above would be modified as follows:

	Before Write-off	After Write-off
Accounts receivable	$200,000	$199,000
Less reserve for doubtful accounts	7,000	6,000
	$193,000	$193,000

Accounting for fixed assets, inventory, cost of goods sold, and bad debts involves the nonfinancial executive in some special problems and aspects of the accounting process. This chapter has attempted to demonstrate that the methods and techniques used by accountants are less difficult and enigmatic than they may seem and that it is important for the nonfinancial executive to understand them.

7

The Basic Accounting Process

ALTHOUGH the primary purpose of this book is to show how to use rather than how to create accounting data, we cannot ignore the latter aspect altogether nor, in fact, should we do so. The nonfinancial executive needs to have at least an elementary understanding of the basic accounting process.

Up to this point, we have described the effect of business transactions simply in terms of increases or decreases in assets, liabilities, and so on. In Chapters 1 and 2, we traced the development of Gerry Manero's Furniture Mart by actually changing the Balance Sheet for the business with each transaction. Although this approach was helpful as background, use of this method to actually account for the business activities of an enterprise of any size would be impractical to the point of impossibility.

More than two centuries ago, merchants devised a much more practical method of double-entry accounting.

The effects of business transactions are collected in records called "accounts." The simplest form of an account is the so-called T account, which, as the name suggests, looks like this:

Every item of financial information that appears on the Balance Sheet and the Income Statement has an account. In all likelihood, there will be many subaccounts for each item; these are "rolled up" and shown as only one figure on a financial statement. The accountant can create an account for any particular item of information he wants to know about the business. For example, he may want to know not only total sales but sales by types of customers such as government, manufacturers, wholesalers, agents, or retailers. To capture this information, he sets up subaccounts under the general sales account. The constraint on setting up accounts, of course, is the increase in the cost and complexity of the accounting system. But no matter how many accounts are set up, they always conform to the general framework of a Balance Sheet and Income Statement. Thus, asset, liability, and owner's equity accounts appear on the Balance Sheet, and revenue, expense, and net income are shown on the Income Statement.

Basic Rules of the Accounting Process

The accounting process involves some basic rules under which accounting data is recorded.

Entry. The recording of a business transaction in an account is referred to as an "accounting entry."

Debits and Credits. An entry on the left-hand side of an account is called a "debit." An entry on the right-hand side is called a "credit." Graphically, this appears in a T form:

T Account	
Debit	Credit
Entry on left-hand side	Entry on right-hand side

When the terms "debit" and "credit" are used in the accounting process, they have no other meaning than the above. This is an important point for the reader to recognize, since "credit" is frequently used with other connotations. These should be ignored when working with the term in accounting.

Balance Sheet and Income Statement accounts increase with debits and credits in accordance with the following immutable rules:

BALANCE SHEET ACCOUNTS

Assets
- Debit entries increase an asset account.
- Credit entries decrease an asset account.

Liabilities
- Debit entries decrease a liability account.
- Credit entries increase a liability account.

Owner's Equity
- Debit entries decrease owner's equity accounts.
- Credit entries increase owner's equity accounts.

INCOME STATEMENT ACCOUNTS

Revenue

- Debit entries decrease revenue accounts.
- Credit entries increase revenue accounts.

Expenses

- Debit entries increase expense accounts.
- Credit entries decrease expense accounts.

Net Income

- Debit entries decrease net income accounts.
- Credit entries increase net income accounts.

These rules are summarized graphically in T account form in Exhibit 7, which shows clearly the logic of the debit-credit mechanism of the accounting process. Note, for example, the relationship between the effects of debits and credits in owner's equity accounts and Income Statement accounts. Owner's equity increases with credits. Revenue, which benefits owner's equity, also increases with credit.

Expenses, we have said, decrease owner's equity. This is done with a debit entry. We can also see that a debit entry to owner's equity also decreases this account.

In previous chapters, we showed that assets decrease as they are consumed, and that through the process of becoming an expense, they reduce owner's equity. Exhibit 7 shows how this would occur through a credit entry to reduce the asset and a debit entry to increase expense (or reduce owner's equity).

Despite the logic of the debit-credit formula, most people (including many practicing accountants) usually find it considerably more practical simply to commit the formula to memory than to think through the logic of every accounting transaction. It is rumored that many a competent accountant has more than once referred to a

Exhibit 7. Double-entry accounting formula.

ASSETS		LIABILITIES	
Dr.	Cr.	Dr.	Cr.
+	−	−	+

		OWNER'S EQUITY	
		Dr.	Cr.
		−	+

REVENUE		EXPENSES	
Dr.	Cr.	Dr.	Cr.
−	+	+	−

NET INCOME	
Dr.	Cr.
−	+

Key
+ = increase
− = decrease

secret formula: "The debits are by the window, the credits are by the door."

A final point, which will not come as a surprise, is that all accounting entries must balance. That is, the debits must always equal the credits. Each particular entry may include two or three elements, but they must in the final sum always be equal to the corresponding debit or credit. This is in keeping with the concept of the Balance Sheet, which requires that assets and equities always be in balance.

Filing Systems

Two instruments are used to file and record accounting data. One of these is the "accounting ledger." We've already discussed the concept of an account. When all the accounts a business uses are grouped together, it is called a ledger; hence the familiar term "company ledger."

The "accounting journal" is the other method. A journal is a log, a document used to record on a daily basis the events that take place. In accounting, the journal is the daily record of the transactions (or events) that occur in the business. Unlike the traveler, who writes in everyday English about the sights and events of his trip, the accountant records his entries in his own particular language of debits and credits. For example, assume that on any given day, just after Gerry Manero has opened his furniture mart, a customer appears and pays a bill. To record this event in the journal, the accountant would want to indicate that the business's cash account had increased and that the accounts receivable from customers had decreased. Using the language of debits and credits, he would make an entry in a journal book which would appear as follows:

> *Debit* Cash
> > *Credit* Accounts receivable

The accountant usually abbreviates the entry in the following form:

> *Dr.* Cash
> > *Cr.* Accounts receivable

This particular entry would probably be the first of many that he would make to record the day's business events in the furniture mart's journal for that day. The process of recording business transactions in this way is called "journalizing" the accounting entry.

Steps of the Accounting Process

Taking the various ideas discussed so far, we can summarize the steps in the accounting process as follows:

1. *Analysis of Transactions.* The first step in established accounting systems in organizations of some size is to assign an account number to a transaction in keeping with the organization's chart of accounts. A chart of accounts is a list of the various categories of expense and income used to accumulate the results of transactions for management control and for operating statements and Balance Sheets. Most charts of account use numbering systems which enable the organization to integrate responsibility reporting systems (in which expenses and, where appropriate, income are associated with a clearly defined organization unit) with financial reporting systems.

Charts of accounts prepared this way are as useful for

periodic reports of performance against budget for the various expense and income categories of organizational units as they are for accumulation of profit center Balance Sheets and operating statements. For example, a chart of accounts may use an account number in the form 22.33.444, in which the first two numbers indicate the major organizational unit; the second two numbers, some significant separable activity of that unit, such as a smaller organizational unit, a special project, or a particular product; and the last three numbers, an expense category such as salaries, travel, telephone and telegraph, and so forth.

With these numbers as the basis, income and expenses can be summarized and totaled by major organization unit, by special project, by expense or income category, by reporting categories typically listed on Balance Sheets and operating statements, or by any of the many possible combinations of these approaches.

Every transaction must be understood and analyzed before it can be accounted for; thus, analysis is the first logical step in the accounting process. In this step, the accountant thinks through the effect of the transaction; that is, as cash increases and accounts receivable decrease, he translates these effects into specific debits and credits to the appropriate accounts—debit cash and credit accounts receivable.

2. *Journalization.* Journalization means the daily recording (in terms of debits and credits to the accounts) of each business transaction. The journal provides the accountant with his daily record of business events.

3. *Posting.* The third step in the accounting process is to transfer, or post, the information that has been recorded in the journal to all the accounts in the ledger.

4. *Adjusting.* Most business transactions take place as

the result of an actual physical act that affects the business. Goods are sold, merchandise is delivered, cash payment is received, assets are purchased, and so on. Most accounting entries originate from such actual business transactions. In addition, however, the accountant needs to adjust the accounting of the business for other factors to present its financial situation accurately. Basically, this involves giving appropriate recognition to reduction in the value of the asset through its use or consumption in the business. Let's take the same two examples we used in exploring this concept in previous chapters.

Assume that the annual amount of the insurance premium of $1,200 was paid in advance. At the time this payment was made, the expenditure created an asset of prepaid insurance. As each month passes, the asset loses some of its value, since the period of coverage is constantly being reduced. On a twelve-month basis, the monthly reduction in value is $100. This fact needs to be reflected in the accounts, which is done by means of an "adjusting entry" that shows the reduction in the value of the asset and the increase in expense by means of the following entry in the journal:

Dr. Insurance expense $100
     Cr. Prepaid assets (insurance) $100

Depreciation is another basic entry that must be made in each accounting period to adjust the accounts of the business. We have discussed the process and rationale used to establish depreciation rates. However, the accountant can reflect these costs in the Income Statement and adjust the value of the fixed assets on the Balance Sheet only if he remembers to make the adjusting entries at the end of the accounting period.

Like other entries, adjusting entries are included in

the journal. They are distinct from entries involving other transactions in that they are triggered only by the mental steps that the accountant takes to accurately adjust the accounts of the business.

5. *Closing.* Earlier we prepared an Income Statement for Gerry Manero by the simple procedure of subtracting the one or two expense transactions from the sum of revenue transactions. Under normal accounting procedure, the revenue and expense accounts of an Income Statement are actually "closed."

To understand the closing step, we must appreciate the fact that there are two types of accounts—real and temporary. Accounts for the Income Statement are temporary, whereas accounts for the Balance Sheet are real. This means that at the end of the accounting period, be it a month or a year, the so-called temporary accounts, or Income Statement accounts, are actually closed out. That is, they are balanced out so that the debit and credit sides are equal, thus making the new opening balance zero. Real accounts, or Balance Sheet accounts, are never closed. They always have a debit or a credit balance.

The closing process involves the steps that are used to take every account that appears on the Income Statement and close it (bring it to zero). The final net income account will then be closed to shareholders' equity account on the Balance Sheet. This is, of course, consistent with the concept that the shareholders' equity account increases with the net income for the accounting period. Later we'll illustrate the accountant's closing procedures with a step-by-step example.

6. *Preparation of Financial Statements.* The final step in the accounting process is preparation of financial statements. This involves extracting information from accounts listed in the company's ledger and presenting it

in accordance with a standard Balance Sheet and Income Statement format.

The Accounting Process Illustrated

Let's turn now to an application of these six steps in the accounting process, again using Gerry Manero's business as the example. In reviewing each transaction, we will start by going through the first three of the six steps required—analysis, journalization, and posting. Once this is done, we will continue to adjust and close the accounts, and then prepare financial statements.

As a first step, we need to confirm the opening balances of our various accounts. To do this, we will look first at Gerry Manero's Balance Sheet:

GERRY MANERO'S FURNITURE MART
Balance Sheet
December 31, 1971

Assets			*Equities*		
			Accounts payable	$100	
Cash	$ 300		Total current liabilities	$ 100	
Accounts receivable	200		Notes payable		2,000
Inventories	3,600		Owner's equity		
Total current assets		$4,100	Capital stock	$5,000	
Fixed assets		5,000	Retained earnings	2,600	
Prepaid assets		600	Total owner's equity		7,600
Total assets		$9,700	Total equities		$9,700

Exhibit 8. Basic general ledger for balance sheet accounts.

ASSETS		EQUITIES	
Dr.	Cr.	Dr.	Cr.
+	−	−	+
CASH		**ACCOUNTS PAYABLE**	
$300			$100
ACCOUNTS RECEIVABLE		**NOTES PAYABLE**	
$200			$2,000
INVENTORIES		**CAPITAL STOCK**	
$3,600			$5,000
FIXED ASSETS		**RETAINED EARNINGS**	
$5,000			$2,600
PREPAID ASSETS			
$600			

The underlying ledger in support of this Balance Sheet appears in Exhibit 8, which shows that there is a ledger account for every item that appears on the Balance Sheet. Moreover, the balances in the ledger accounts correspond to the amounts shown on the Balance Sheet. Since Balance Sheet accounts are never closed, they always reflect a credit or debit balance unless there is nothing of value to be recorded in the account.

We might note one further point. In the ledger, the account cash shows a balance of $300. We know that cash is an asset, and that assets are increased with a debit and decreased with a credit. Since the converse is true for liabilities, we expect the values shown in these accounts to be reflected as credits on the right-hand side of the account, as they are in Exhibit 8.

Exhibit 9 shows the so-called temporary or Income Statement accounts for the furniture mart. Note that none of these shows a balance, since they are temporary accounts and have a balance of zero from the closing of the last accounting period.

Now to our detailed application of the steps in the accounting process. Each transaction described below has a corresponding entry in Exhibit 10, and Transactions 6 and 7 appear in both Exhibit 10 and Exhibit 11.

Transaction 1. Customer pays $100 to the furniture mart, settling an outstanding accounts receivable.

Step 1, analysis of transaction. As a result of this transaction, the company has received $100 in cash. The asset cash increases by this amount, and the asset accounts receivable decreases by the same amount.

Step 2, journalization. The formal accounting treatment of this transaction in the journal would be shown:

Dr. Cash $100
    Cr. Accounts receivable $100

Exhibit 9. Basic general ledger for income statement accounts.

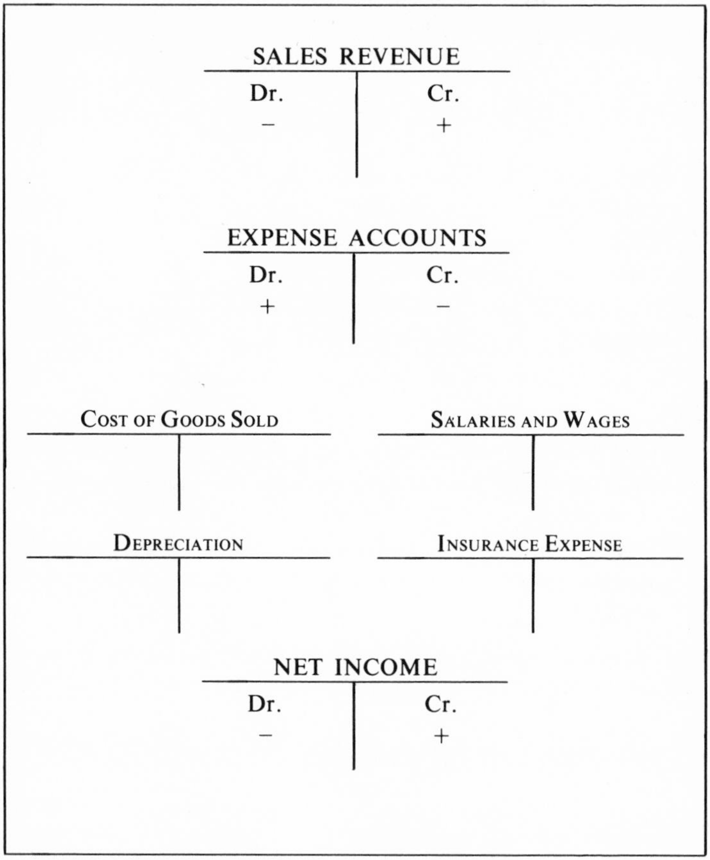

Exhibit 10. Cumulative postings of balance sheet accounts.

ASSETS		EQUITIES	
Dr.	Cr.	Dr.	Cr.
+	–	–	+

CASH		ACCOUNTS PAYABLE	
$300*			$100*
†(1) $100	$100 (2)	(2) $100	
(3) 5,000	2,000 (4)		
(6) 3,000	1,000 (5)		
	600 (7)		

ACCOUNTS RECEIVABLE		NOTES PAYABLE	
$200			$2,000*
	$100 (1)	(4) $2,000	

INVENTORIES		CAPITAL STOCK	
$3,600*			$5,000*
(5) 1,000	$2,000 (6)		5,000 (3)

FIXED ASSETS		RETAINED EARNINGS	
$5,000*			$2,600*
	$50 adjusting entry		300

PREPAID ASSETS	
$600*	
	$50 adjusting entry

*Indicates opening balance
†Numbers in parentheses indicate transactions

Exhibit 11. Cumulative postings of income statement accounts.

```
                        SALES REVENUE
                  ────────────────────────────
                  Dr.           │   Cr.
                   −            │    +
                                │  $3,000  (6)*
                                │
                                │
                                │
                                │

                      EXPENSE  ACCOUNTS
                  ────────────────────────────
                  Dr.           │   Cr.
                   +            │    −
                                │
                                │
                                │

     COST OF GOODS SOLD                    SALARIES AND WAGES
  ──────────────────────              ──────────────────────
  *(6)  $2,000  │                     (7)  $600   │
                │                                 │
                │                                 │

      DEPRECIATION                         INSURANCE EXPENSE
  ──────────────────────              ──────────────────────
   $50†         │                      $50†        │
                │                                 │
                │                                 │

                        NET  INCOME
                  ────────────────────────────
                  Dr.           │   Cr.
                   −            │    +
                                │
                                │
                                │
```

Key
    *Numbers in parentheses indicate transactions.
    †Adjusting entry.

Step 3, posting. The transaction would be posted to the T accounts in the ledger as follows:

CASH	
Dr.	Cr.
+	−
$100	

ACCOUNTS RECEIVABLE	
	$100

Transaction 2. The furniture mart pays $100 to a creditor, settling an account.

Step 1, analysis of transaction. The asset cash has been decreased by $100. At the same time a liability in the amount of $100, which was previously an account payable, has been reduced by the same amount.

Step 2, journalization.

Dr. Accounts payable $100
    Cr. Cash $100

Step 3, posting. The transaction would be posted to the T accounts in the ledger as follows:

CASH		ACCOUNTS PAYABLE	
Dr.	Cr.	Dr.	Cr.
+	−	−	+
	$100	$100	

Transaction 3. The furniture mart issues stock for a value of $5,000 to various members of the Manero family, receiving cash.

Step 1, analysis of transaction. The company has received $5,000 in cash, and the amount of this asset is increased by $5,000. At the same time, shareholders' equity has been increased since the stock was the source of these funds. That asset also increases by $5,000.

Step 2, journalization.

Dr. Cash $5,000
          Cr. Owner's equity (capital stock) $5,000

Step 3, posting. This transaction would be posted to the T accounts in the ledger as follows:

CASH		OWNER'S EQUITY	
Dr.	Cr.	Dr.	Cr.
+	–	–	+
$5,000			$5,000

Transaction 4. The furniture mart uses some of the proceeds it received from its stock issue to pay off its $2,000 note payable.

Step 1, analysis of transaction. The company has reduced its asset cash in the amount of $2,000. At the same time it has reduced a liability to a creditor, or a claim on its assets, by the same $2,000.

Step 2, journalization.

Dr. Notes payable $2,000
          Cr. Cash $2,000

Step 3, posting. This transaction would be posted to the T accounts of the ledger as follows:

CASH		NOTES PAYABLE	
Dr.	Cr.	Dr.	Cr.
+	–	–	+
	$2,000	$2,000	

Transaction 5. The company purchases merchandise for $1,000 in cash.

Step 1, analysis of transaction. The company has increased one of its assets, merchandise. At the same time, it has used another asset to make this purchase, cash, which has to be decreased.

Step 2, journalization.

Dr. Merchandise inventory $1,000
    Cr. Cash $1,000

Step 3, posting. This transaction would be posted to the T accounts of the general ledger as follows:

CASH

Dr.	Cr.
+	−
	$1,000

INVENTORIES

$1,000	

Transaction 6. The furniture mart sells merchandise for $3,000 cash that cost $2,000.

Step 1, analysis of transaction. Several things have happened because of this transaction. It is the first event to affect the Income Statement, since the company has delivered merchandise and thereby obtained increased revenue. At the same time, because the merchandise was sold for cash, this asset is increased. In exchange, the furniture mart turns over merchandise that cost $2,000, decreasing the value of its inventory by this amount. This increases its expense, cost of goods sold, by the same amount.

Step 2, journalization. Journal entries for this transaction, because it involves several accounts, are four:

Dr. Cash $3,000
    Cr. Revenue (Exhibit 11) $3,000

Dr. Cost of goods sold (Exhibit 11) $2,000
    Cr. Merchandise Inventory (Exhibit 10). $2,000

Step 3, posting. This transaction would be posted to the T accounts of the general ledger as follows:

BALANCE SHEET ACCOUNTS (Exhibit 10)

CASH

Dr.	Cr.
+	–
$3,000	

INVENTORIES

Dr.	Cr.
+	–
	$2,000

INCOME STATEMENT ACCOUNTS (Exhibit 11)

REVENUE

Dr.	Cr.
–	+
	$3,000

COST OF GOODS SOLD

Dr.	Cr.
+	–
$2,000	

Transaction 7. The furniture mart pays $600 of salaries and wages in cash.

Step 1, analysis of transaction. The asset, cash, decreases by $600; the expense, salaries and wages, increases by the same amount.

Step 2, journalization.

Dr. Expenses (salaries and wages; Exhibit 11) . . $600
    Cr. Cash (Exhibit 10) $600

Step 3, posting. This transaction would be posted to the T accounts of the general ledger as follows:

BALANCE SHEET

Cash	
Dr.	Cr.
+	–
	$600

INCOME STATEMENT

Salaries and Wages	
Dr.	Cr.
+	–
$600	

For the preceding seven transactions, we have carried out the first three steps involved in the accounting process —analysis, journalization, and posting. We should again make clear that the posting has been done at the same time as both of the other steps. However, in actual practice, the journal would probably be posted to the company's ledger as a separate step, later in the day or even at the end of the week or the month.

Adjusting

We noted earlier that at the end of each accounting period it is necessary to think through the adjustments that need to be made to accurately reflect the status of the business. Usually these adjustments involve recognition of expense that arises from the use of an asset during the accounting period under consideration.

In our case, there are fixed assets of $5,000 and prepaid assets of $600. The fixed asset consists of a Volkswagen delivery van for which we shall assume an annual depreciation cost of $600. Prepaid assets consist of a prepaid insurance premium.

If we assume, for the sake of simplicity, that the business transactions have spanned the period of a month, the values of both these assets need to be adjusted (with a corresponding expense increase) to reflect their usage during this period.

In the case of the Volkswagen, if the annual rate of depreciation is $600, then the monthly rate is $50. The accountant needs to reflect a decrease in the value of fixed assets of this amount and a corresponding increase in expense. We said earlier that rather than entering a direct deduction from the value of fixed assets, the accountant uses a reserve for depreciation. We, however, shall simply make the entry directly to fixed assets. The depreciation adjustment for the month of January 1971 would result in the following journal entries:

> *Dr.* Depreciation expense. $50
>   *Cr.* Fixed assets $50

The transaction would be posted to T accounts of the general ledger as follows:

BALANCE SHEET

FIXED ASSETS

Dr.	Cr.
+	−
	$50

INCOME STATEMENT

DEPRECIATION EXPENSES

Dr.	Cr.
+	−
$50	

The prepaid asset consists of an annual insurance premium that has been paid in advance. Its value also decreases at a rate of $50 per month, with adjusting entries that would appear in journal form as follows:

Dr. Insurance expense $50
   Cr. Prepaid assets
      Insurance $50

Posting to T accounts in the ledger, we have

BALANCE SHEET

PREPAID ASSETS

Dr.	Cr.
+	−
	$50

INCOME STATEMENT

INSURANCE EXPENSE

Dr.	Cr.
+	−
$50	

The reader will note that although we have listed the adjusting step as a separate phase of the accounting process, it also involves analysis as well as journalization of the appropriate accounting entries.

The Closing Process

We said earlier that the Income Statement accounts were temporary accounts which had to be closed at the end of each accounting period. This closing involved taking each account and establishing the debit or credit entry that was necessary to bring the account to a zero balance. The following step-by-step procedure will more clearly illustrate this logical process.

Closing the Revenue Account

Exhibit 11 is the Income Statement of the furniture mart, with the entries of the transactions posted to each of the T accounts. The first account is revenue, which has a credit balance of $3,000. If we want this account to equal zero, or close it out, we must debit for $3,000. We want to close the revenue account to the net income account so the other half of the entry would be a credit to net income, thus:

> *Dr.* Revenue $3,000
>   *Cr.* Net income $3,000

Closing the Expense Accounts

The next step is to close the expense accounts to net income. The first of these is cost of goods sold, which has a debit balance of $2,000. To close it, we must make a credit entry of $2,000. That is, the balancing debit portion of the entry must be to net income for the same amount, thus:

> *Dr.* Net income. $2,000
>   *Cr.* Cost of goods sold. $2,000

The net expense account is salaries and wages, which also has a debit balance of $600. To be closed, it must also have a credit entry of $600, thus:

> *Dr.* Net income. $600
>   *Cr.* Salaries and wages $600

The depreciation and insurance accounts show a balance of $50 each. They would receive exactly the same treatment as the other two expense accounts, and we would have:

> *Dr.* Net income $50
>   *Cr.* Depreciation expense. $50

> *Dr.* Net income $50
>   *Cr.* Insurance expense $50

Closing the Net Income Account

All the accounts in the Income Statement have been closed except for the final one, net income. It, too, must be closed. By adding the debits and credits, we can see that there is a debit balance of $2,700 and a credit balance of $3,000.

To close the account, we must make a debit entry of $300. The other half of the entry is to be a credit to owner's equity. In formal form:

> *Dr.* Net income. $300
>   *Cr.* Owner's equity (retained earnings, Exhibit 10) . . $300

Throughout the closing process, and particularly in this last step, we can see the consistent relationship between the mechanics of the accounting process and the basic accounting concepts. The credit to owner's equity

GERRY MANERO'S FURNITURE MART
Balance Sheet
January 31, 1971

Assets			Equities	
Cash	$4,700			
Accounts receivable	100			
			Accounts payable	0
Inventories	2,600		Notes payable	0
Current assets		$ 7,400		
			Owner's equity	
Fixed assets	$4,950		Capital stock	$10,000
Prepaid assets	550	5,500	Retained earnings	2,900
Total assets		$12,900	Total equities	$12,900

GERRY MANERO'S FURNITURE MART
Income Statement
For Period Ending January 31, 1971

Sales revenue	$3,000
Less cost of goods sold	2,000
Gross margin	$1,000
Less	
Salaries and wages	600
Depreciation expense	50
Insurance expense	50
Total expenses	700
Net income	$ 300

in the closing of the net income account is, of course, an increase—which is exactly how we described the function of the Income Statement in conceptual terms.

Preparation of Financial Statements

The final step in the accounting process is the preparation of financial statements. To do this, we simply take the balances that appear in the ledger of accounts for the Balance Sheet and Income Statement and cast them into the conventional format for both these statements. Examples are shown at left.

We have worked with only a few very simple business transactions to account for Gerry Manero's efforts. The point should be made, however, that the principles, procedures, and processes discussed in this chapter and employed in the last several illustrations are exactly those that an accountant would use, no matter how numerous or complex the transactions. Stripped of its jargon, the basic accounting process is rather logical and simple.

8

Manufacturing
Cost Essentials

So far we have dealt only with the concepts and procedures involved in accounting for business transactions which involve the purchase and resale of merchandise. Since there are well over 311,000 manufacturing firms in the United States, according to the most recent statistics of the National Association of Manufacturers, it would be unrealistic to ignore altogether any discussion of manufacturing cost accounting.

At the same time, we should recognize that manufacturing cost accounting, or "cost accounting," as it is usually called, is a subject unto itself and worthy of treatment in one, if not several, books. In this chapter we shall discuss only some fundamental concepts, particularly those that will lead to a better understanding of the financial results of a manufacturing enterprise.

Merchandising Versus Manufacturing

Merchandising is a rather simple, straightforward process. It involves the purchase and ultimate resale of a product. Gerry Manero, as well as the local merchants with whom we all deal, is a merchandiser or merchant.

The manufacturer differs from the merchandiser in that he makes the product he sells. This involves either conversion or fabrication which starts with some form of a raw material that is subjected to a manufacturing process requiring either machinery or labor, and probably both. Let us suppose that the EZI Manufacturing Company is involved with the manufacture of widgets. The firm has determined that it costs $10 to make a widget. This consists of:

- *Material:* $5 for the cost of the raw material.
- *Labor:* $3 for the cost of the labor for the time involved in making the widget.
- *Factory overhead:* $2 for the general costs of the factory in which the widget is manufactured. This would include heat, light, power, janitorial services, and similar expenses.

In most cases, accounting for the manufacturing costs of material and labor is not unduly difficult. Factory overhead is where the wicket, or if you will, the widget, gets a bit sticky. To see why this is so, let's look at Exhibit 12, which shows the categories of costs the accountant must work with.

Of the five basic types of costs shown in Exhibit 12, the first three—labor, material, and factory overhead—are unique to the manufacturer. The last two, general administrative and selling expenses, are common to manufacturers and merchandisers. In manufacturing

Exhibit 12. Cost elements and their accounting treatment.

Cost Elements	Cost of Merchandiser	Cost of Manufacturer	Clear-Cut Product Costs	Clear-Cut Period Costs	Period and Product Cost	Accounting Treatment
Direct labor		X	X			Product
Direct material		X	X			Product
Factory overhead		X			X	Product — some division made as to product vs. period
General and administrative expense	X	X			X	Period
Selling expense	X	X		X		Period

cost accounting, the problem arises because the difference between expenses which are factory overhead and those which are listed under general and administrative expenses is often fuzzy.

Assume, for example, that EZI Manufacturing Company has a large factory in which it manufactures widgets. The same building contains offices for the general manager, the accounting staff, the purchasing department, the engineering control group, and the sales department. Just one of the accountant's problems is to determine how all the costs associated with this building—taxes, insurance, heat and power, and so on—are to be divided between the factory overhead categories of general and administrative expenses and selling expenses. To be sure, this division of costs is by no means impossible, but since the costs are common to all these activities, there are no correct scientific delineations. This is only one example, but once we appreciate the difficulty of precise identification of factory overhead expenses, we can turn to the consequences of this problem.

Period Versus Product Expenses

Returning to Exhibit 12, we can see that five general categories of costs have been separated into two broad groups—product expenses and period expenses.

Product expenses, as the name suggests, are those costs which vary with each product made. Direct material is an excellent example. We have said that there is $5 of material in every widget; every time another widget is made, the expenses for the accounting period in which it was made increases $5. Labor is also generally considered to be a product cost. It may not always vary as directly with production as does material cost, but like material costs it can be directly identified with the manufacture of the product.

Period costs generally can be thought of as overhead costs. They consist, as the exhibit shows, of general administrative and selling expenses. Period costs derive their name from the fact that they occur over a period of time, regardless of the volume of goods produced or sold. For example, the property taxes on the factory in which the EZI Company manufactures widgets obviously do not increase with each additional widget that is manufactured. The same would be true for insurance. Selling expenses, too, do not necessarily depend on the number of units manufactured but rather on the sales effort. These indirect costs can only be assigned to a period of time by the accountant, usually on the basis of when they were incurred.

As Exhibit 12 illustrates, there is a gray area between the clear-cut period costs and product costs. That area includes many types of expenses which are not readily identifiable as one or the other. In reality, they are probably a bit of both. Despite this fact, in manufacturing accounting the accountant must make a delineation. It is even more important to understand that the manner in which this delineation is made (and it always must be made) can have a profound influence on the net income that is reported for the business.

Let's explore this proposition more specifically, recalling the accounting life cycle of converting assets to expenses. As an asset is consumed in the business, it becomes an expense. When goods are purchased, they become an asset, inventory. At the time of sale, when they are turned over to the customer, they become an expense, cost of goods sold.

The manufacturer also carries inventories; however, he makes rather than purchases his inventories. The values that he assigns to his inventories and his cost of goods sold are what it has cost him to make the product. The costs to make a manufactured product are those of material, labor, and factory overhead.

We have seen, however, that in practice there is considerable imprecision in differentiating between factory overhead and general and administrative expenses. If the accountant decides that some of the expenses in the gray area between period costs and product costs are in fact product costs, then these costs are reflected as part of the value of the manufacturer's inventory. Thus, *they are shown as an asset rather than as an expense until the products are sold.* If, conversely, the accountant decides that the expense in question is a period expense, *it is shown as an expense for the accounting period rather than as an asset.*

To illustrate this phenomenon, let's look at XYZ Tool Machinery, Inc., and at the dramatically different financial results that company can obtain from the same manufacturing costs—depending on the decisions it makes regarding period versus product costs.

XYZ Tool Machinery, Inc.
Production for Period: Five Units (Machine Tools)
Sales for Period: Three Units (Machine Tools)

Costs to Produce Five Units

Labor	$250,000
Material	200,000
Overhead Factory General and administrative	} 500,000
Selling	100,000

The distinction between factory expenses and general and administrative expenses is unclear. In Case A (see Exhibit 13) the accountant assumes that 80 percent of overhead costs are product costs. In Case B he assumes that only 50 percent of the overhead costs are product

Exhibit 13. Calculation of inventory unit costs and general and administrative expenses.

| | COST OF GOODS SOLD | | | |
| | Case A | | Case B | |
	Total	Per Unit	Total	Per Unit
Labor	$250,000	$ 50,000	$250,000	$ 50,000
Materials	200,000	40,000	200,000	40,000
Overhead				
80% × $500,000	400,000	80,000		
50% × $500,000			250,000	50,000
Totals	$850,000	$170,000	$700,000	$140,000

GENERAL AND ADMINISTRATIVE EXPENSES

	Case A	Case B

Overhead
  Factory
  General and
  administrative
	$500,000	$500,000

Designated as factory overhead	$400,000	$250,000

Balance, designated
  as general and
  administrative
  expense for the
  period
	$100,000	$250,000

Exhibit 14. Calculation of net income.

	Case A		Case B	
	Per Unit	*Total*	*Per Unit*	*Total*
Sales revenue (3 units)	$250,000	$750,000	$250,000	$750,000
Less cost of goods sold (3 units)	170,000	510,000	140,000	420,000
Gross margin	$ 80,000	$240,000	$110,000	$330,000
Selling expense		100,000		100,000
General and administrative expenses		100,000		250,000
Net income/loss before taxes		40,000		(20,000)
Value of inventory shown on balance sheet at end of accounting period (2 units)		$340,000		$280,000

costs. With these assumptions, the calculation for the cost of goods sold and inventories for the period would be as shown in Exhibit 13.

The net income for the period, on the basis of the sales of three units of machine tools at a price of $250,000 per unit, would appear as in Exhibit 14.

We will leave unanswered the question as to whether the company made or lost money. In practice and with a great deal more information, accountants could undoubtedly arrive at a consensus. In fact, they do, since some choice must be made between period and product costs to determine the net income of a manufacturer. The convention of consistency, which would require that the same approach be used from one accounting period to another, can be of assistance in making manufacturing cost calculations more meaningful over an extended period. Still, the choice is less than scientific and can be significant. No one can make intelligent use of the accounting and financial data of a manufacturing organization without recognizing this fact.

Three Manufacturing Cost Systems

Basic as they may be, the concepts and issues we have discussed provide sufficient background for a brief and general discussion of three different types of manufacturing cost systems: absorption cost systems, direct cost systems, and standard cost systems.

Absorption Cost Systems

Another name for absorption costing is "full costing." In this system, all three elements of manufacturing costs—direct labor, direct material, and factory overhead—are absorbed and charged to the product. In this manner, all the manufacturing costs are totally absorbed and figure as product expense, and none of them is taken as a period cost.

Absorption costing is the most conventional approach to manufacturing cost accounting, and the cost of goods sold that appears in the Income Statement of almost any major corporate manufacturing concern uses this method. The full absorption approach enables us to know that inventory values on the Balance Sheet include an element of factory overhead which will not be reflected as an expense in the Income Statement until the product is sold. In the preceding section, we discussed some of the difficulties and implications of defining factory overhead costs which must be assigned to the product under the absorption costing system.

Direct Costing Systems

Absorption cost accounting systems are used, and in fact are mandatory, for governmental as well as public financial reporting. In recent years, however, the continuing emphasis on the use of accounting data for management purposes has brought into being an alternative method of manufacturing cost accounting, which is called "direct cost accounting." This method is almost always used exclusively for internal purposes, and is therefore employed in addition to absorption cost accounting.

In direct cost accounting only those elements that can be clearly and directly identified with the manufacture of each product are charged as the cost of that product, usually only direct material and labor. Thus the subtleties and vagaries of allocating overhead between products and periods are totally avoided.

The effect of direct versus absorption cost accounting is illustrated in Exhibit 15, which shows that under direct costing the elements of manufacturing overhead are not charged to the product but rather to the period in which they were incurred. When this approach is used, net income for the period more directly corresponds to the sales activity. This particular aspect of direct costing is one of the major attractions to its advocates, who argue that in fact it is much more accurate to have net income respond to sales. They further argue that the whole process of overhead determination and allocation to products is of necessity fuzzy and difficult. Therefore, nothing is really served by the whole process, since it tends to cloud rather than to clarify financial results.

Exhibit 15. Direct versus absorption cost accounting.

	Accounting Period 1	Accounting Period 2
Production in units	5	5
Sales in units	3	7
Sales price per unit	$250,000	$250,000
Costs		
Labor		250,000
Material		200,000
Factory overhead*		250,000
General and administrative expenses		250,000
Selling		100,000

*Factory overhead and general and administrative expenses have been distributed as per Case B in Exhibit 14.

FACTORY OVERHEAD UNIT COST

Period	Total Factory Overhead Cost	Units Produced	Factory Overhead Per Unit
1	$250,000	5	$50,000
2	250,000	5	50,000

Unit Cost	Absorption	Direct
Labor	$ 50,000	$50,000
Material	40,000	40,000
Factory overhead	50,000	0
Totals	$140,000	$90,000

CIRCULATION COSTS OF GOODS SOLD

Period	Sales Units	Absorption Costs Per Unit	Absorption Costs For Period	Direct Costs Per Unit	Direct Costs For Period
1	3	$140,000	$ 420,000	$90,000	$270,000
2	7	140,000	980,000	90,000	630,000
Totals	10		$1,400,000		$900,000

Exhibit 15 continued.

Table showing comparative income statement for EZI Company.

| | Absorption Costing | | Direct Costing | |
	Period 1	Period 2	Period 1	Period 2
Sales				
Units	3	7	3	7
Revenue	$750,000	$1,750,000	$750,000	$1,750,000
Less				
Labor	150,000	350,000	150,000	350,000
Material	120,000	280,000	120,000	280,000
Factory overhead	150,000	350,000	0	0
Cost of goods sold	420,000	980,000	270,000	630,000
Less				
Gross margin	$330,000	$ 770,000	$480,000	$1,120,000
Factory overhead	0	0	250,000	250,000
Selling expenses	100,000	100,000	100,000	100,000
General and administrative expenses	250,000	250,000	250,000	250,000
Total expenses	$350,000	$ 350,000	$600,000	$ 600,000
Net income/(loss)	(20,000)	420,000	(120,000)	520,000
Cumulative net income	$400,000		$400,000	
Finding inventory				
Units	2	0	2	0
Value				

Furthermore, as we can see, the amount of overhead that gets charged under absorption costing will depend on the physical volume of units that are manufactured. This figure can give a higher or lower cost per unit of manufacture but tends to be somewhat misleading, since the total amount of overhead costs will not have varied. For all these reasons, more and more businesses are now using direct manufacturing cost accounting systems for internal managerial control and decision purposes.

Standard Cost Systems

Like direct costing, the concepts of standard costing grew out of the continuing search for a more effective use of accounting data for managerial purposes. Throughout our discussion of manufacturing costs, we have been thinking in terms of the costs as they were incurred and recorded in the accounting records of a manufacturing enterprise. This is historical cost data and only tells management what costs were. The idea behind standard costing, however, is to provide management with information as to what costs should be, rather than simply what they were.

By definition, "standard" implies a bench mark or a yardstick of performance. Since standard costs are meant to serve as a criterion for efficiency rather than simply to register what has actually happened, they must be well thought out and accurate. More often than not, they are engineered; that is to say, they are determined after a thorough and scientific investigation of what costs should be incurred to manufacture a product.

In the EZI Company's manufacture of widgets, for example, a standard costing system would be developed in conjunction with engineers who would, after analysis and time and motion studies, determine that a certain amount of money should be spent for raw materials for each product, and a certain amount of overhead should be incurred. These three elements in total would then represent what should happen if the product is manufactured under efficient, well-managed conditions. Once this system is determined, all that is required is to record the total physical number of units manufactured during a given period, and then to apply the standard cost rate to this volume of production. This, then, is the total shown as the standard cost of manufacture. Sometimes standard costs are built up on the basis of past experience and cost data rather than predetermined through engineering studies.

Under a standard costing system, the procedures involved in the recording of actual costs are not discontinued. Actual costs incurred are also accounted for. They can then be compared against the standard costs, and the difference can be shown as a variance. A variance can either be favorable or unfavorable. If actual costs are less than those established in the standard costing system, the variance is favorable; if actual costs are higher, the variance is unfavorable. Exhibit 16 shows how the net income for XYZ Tool Machinery, Inc., might be recorded under a standard costing system.

The appeal of the standard costing system is obvious. It facilitates management's evaluation as to whether or not the manufacturing process is being carried on efficiently. By providing a continuing gauge of efficiency, it allows management to take action when necessary to correct a problem or inefficiency more quickly. Also, use of the system can often actually facilitate and simplify the accounting process. This is particularly true in the manufacture of high-volume items, where it becomes extremely

Exhibit 16. Income statement of XYZ Tool Machinery, Inc.

Sales	$2,500,000
Less	
Cost of goods sold at standard rate	$1,400,000
Variances *unfavorable*	200,000
Cost of goods sold	$1,600,000
Gross profit	$ 900,000
Less	
Selling expenses	200,000
General and administrative expenses	500,000
Net income before taxes	$ 200,000
Variances	
Material variance (higher cost)	$ 100,000
Labor variance (higher cost)	100,000

difficult to record on an actual basis the cost of manufacture for each unit. It is important to recognize, however, that the final net income must always be based on the actual costs incurred and not the standard cost. A standard costing system can involve standards for only direct costs and/or direct plus full costs. In other words, a standard costing system can be a direct standard costing system or a standard absorption costing system.

9

Fundamentals of
Financial Analysis

To begin, let us assume nothing and ask the basic question: Why financial analysis? The following earnings results were obtained by one company in 1971:

Earnings per share	55¢
Sales	$33,667,319
Net income	$859,523

This information is not extensive, but it does include the key data from an Income Statement. Still, it's hard to draw a conclusion. Is the fact that the corporation earned 55 cents per share in 1971 good or bad? We need to stop and ask: What are the basic objectives of a business?

In his recent and controversial book, *The New Industrial State,* Galbraith suggests that the basic purpose of a good portion of large American business is to perpetuate a network of jobs that continues to employ and amuse corporate technicians and bureaucrats.[1] A contrary and more conventional answer was offered in a speech by William Howlett, president of Consolidated Foods Corporation. He stated that profit is the basic objective of a business, profit not only in the sense of net income but also as an acronym for "Proper Return on Funds Invested Today (and Tomorrow)."

Although income and adequacy of return on invested funds are the sine qua non of business endeavor, there are also other considerations, namely, that bills must be paid.

R. N. Anthony succinctly summarizes these ideas with the statement: "The overall objective of a business is to earn a satisfactory return on the funds invested in it, consistent with maintaining a sound financial position."[2]

With these thoughts in mind, we return to our original question: Why financial analysis? The answer is: Financial analysis provides procedures to facilitate the measurement and evaluation of a business firm's progress toward accomplishment of general business objectives, to wit, earning a satisfactory return and maintaining a satisfactory financial position. Let's explore these objectives in greater detail.

Return on Investment

The concept of earning a satisfactory return on investment has its origin in classical economic theory, which states that capital is entitled to a return for its use. The earnings of a business may be large or small; they may

---

[1] John Kenneth Galbraith, *The New Industrial State* (Boston: Houghton Mifflin, 1967).

[2] R. N. Anthony, *Management Accounting Principles* (Homewood, Ill.: Richard D. Irwin, 1965).

increase or decrease, but when all is said and done, the income of the enterprise really tells us very little unless we know how much investment was required to generate this income.

Perhaps we can better appreciate the importance of this idea if we think of it in personal terms. Suppose we are approached by an entrepreneur who says, "I can guarantee you $3,000 a year if you'll make an investment with me." Obviously, we are not going to make this investment until we understand its magnitude. If the proposed investment is $300,000, we are obviously contemplating something less than a bonanza. On the other hand, if it's $30,000, the return appears to be more in line with the investment.

Proper return on funds invested is perhaps the key criterion of a successful business undertaking. In modern management usage, return on investment (ROI) is now used by itself as a management tool. One of the major objectives of financial analysis is to measure the success a business has in obtaining an adequate return on investment.

Financial Condition

The second major criterion for success is maintenance of a satisfactory financial condition. This usually involves two aspects—a short-term financial position and an adequate long-term position—or, to describe it differently, adequate liquidity and adequate solvency. "Liquidity" is the ability of a business to meet its short-term financial obligations promptly and satisfactorily. "Solvency" is its ability to meet its longer-term financial obligations.

The techniques of financial analysis can be broken down into three logical groups that measure and evaluate each of these parameters: financial analysis which measures liquidity, that which measures solvency, and that which measures corporate profitability and return on invested funds.

Ratios are the primary method used for financial analysis. A ratio is simply the mathematical relationship of one number to another. Percentages are the expression of a number when the base is 100. Let's look now at some specific applications of ratios and percentages in three areas of financial analysis. We will use the financial data that appears in the Balance Sheet and Income Statement of XYZ Tool Machinery, Inc., as shown in Exhibit 17.

Liquidity Analysis

Liquidity is the ability of a corporation to meet its current obligations, which, you will recall, are so-called current assets. These appear as the first major category on the left-hand side of the Balance Sheet. They are ranked in the order of their liquidity, beginning with the item of "cash." On the right-hand side of the Balance Sheet the converse of current assets is "liabilities," which are ordinarily ranked in order of the immediacy of their payment.

Current assets are, by definition, either cash or will be converted to cash in the course of a year. Current liabilities are those which are due and payable within a year. Under normal circumstances, a business would use its current assets to pay its current liabilities, since both of them are involved in an annual receivable payment cycle.

Current Ratio

The first, and one of the most common, ratios which measures this relationship is called the "current ratio." It

Exhibit 17. Balance sheet and income statement for XYZ Tool Machinery, Inc.

BALANCE SHEET
($000)
December 31, 1971

	1970	1971			1970	1971
Current assets						
Cash	$ 40	$ 50				
Accounts receivable	50	60	*Current liabilities*			
Inventory	70	60	Accounts payable	$ 40	$ 50	
Prepaid expenses	20	20	Accrued wages	20	30	
Total current assets	$180	$190	Accrued taxes	30	20	
Fixed assets			Total current liabilities	$ 90	$100	
Property, plant, and equipment	$150	$183	*Long-term liabilities*			
			Bonds payable	70	70	
Less accumulated depreciation	70	80	Total liabilities	$ 70	$ 70	
			Shareholders' equity			
Net property, plant, and equipment	80	103	Common stock	60	60	
			Retained earnings	50	73	
Total fixed assets	$ 80	$103	Total shareholders' equity	$110	$133	
Other assets	10	10				
Total assets	$270	$303	Total equities	$270	$303	

INCOME STATEMENT
For Period Ending 1971

Sales	$400,000
Less cost of goods sold	280,000
Gross profit	$120,000
Less selling expenses	50,000
Less administrative expenses	20,000
Operating income	$ 50,000
Interest expense	4,200
Income before taxes	$ 45,800
Income taxes	22,800
Net income after taxes	$ 23,000

is obtained by dividing the current assets of a business by its current liabilities and would be calculated from the 1971 figures for XYZ Tool Machinery, Inc.'s Balance Sheet in Exhibit 17 as follows:

$$\frac{\text{Current assets}}{\text{Current liabilities}} = \frac{190}{100} = 1.9 \text{ current ratio}$$

We can interpret the current ratio of the company as follows: It has $1.90 of current assets to meet $1.00 of debt due as a current liability.

In using ratios for financial analysis, each individual situation must be considered. However, as a general rule, a current ratio of 2 to 1 is considered to be quite healthy in American business practices.

Quick Ratio

Current assets include usually three basic items—cash, accounts receivable, and inventories. When we evaluate the liquidity of a company on the basis of its current ratio, we assume that the inventory which figures as part of the total current assets is liquid. However, this assumption may not always be realistic. For example, obsolete merchandise may appear as an item of inventory but in fact have no value whatsoever. Or, in the same way, inventory may be represented by several large items, such as a boat in the case of a marina, which would not necessarily become liquid in a short period of time.

For this reason, a second and more stringent evaluation of a company's liquidity can be obtained by the so-called quick ratio, or what is sometimes called the "acid test ratio." The quick ratio is computed by taking the "quick" assets of a corporation, which are defined as cash and accounts receivable, and relating them to the total current liabilities of the corporation. Using the figures from XYZ Tool Machinery's Balance Sheet, the quick ratio appears as shown below:

Cash	$ 50	
Accounts receivable	60	
Quick assets	$110	= 1.1 quick ratio
Current liabilities	$100	

The company has a quick ratio of 1.1 to 1. That is, there is $1.10 of quick assets that can be used to meet the payments of current liabilities. The results of this particular quick ratio indicate that if the company were really pressed and were not able to quickly sell the merchandise that it holds in inventory, it would still be able to meet all its current obligations out of both its cash and accounts receivable. As a general rule of thumb, a quick ratio of 1.1 to 1 is generally considered adequate. However, once again we need to be careful in making generalizations, since the unique aspects of each individual situation surrounding a particular company's business must be considered.

Although the quick or acid test ratio subjects the company to a much more rigorous evaluation of its liquidity, the quick assets include the accounts receivable of the business. Therefore, the ratio implicitly assumes that the accounts receivable are readily collectible and in fact have liquidity. Under normal conditions, we would expect this to be the case.

We can, however, specifically evaluate the collectibility of a business's accounts receivable by determining the relationship of receivables to the total annual sales. The receivable data is available from the Balance Sheet and the annual sales data appears on the Income Statement.

Average Collection Period

The numbers from XYZ Tool Machinery indicate that receivables at year end 1971 of $60,000 are 15 percent of the total annual sales of $400,000 for the company in 1971. Total sales of the company were made over the period of a year, or 365 days. If the accounts receivable represent 15 percent of annual sales in terms of dollars, they also represent 15 percent of the 365 days over which they were made. Fifteen percent of 365 days equals 55 days (rounded). This means that on the average, the company takes 55 days to collect its accounts receivable. On an individual basis, some of these accounts receivable will be collected in a shorter period of time, and others in a longer period of time. As an overall average, however, 55 calendar days pass before an account receivable is collected and becomes cash. This is often referred to as "the average collection period."

The calculation of this period, as shown above, helps evaluate the liquidity of a company's accounts receivable. If the results for XYZ Tool Machinery resulted in an average collection period of 180 days, we would, of course, have a different assessment of the speed with which the accounts receivable could be liquidated to obtain cash for the payment of current liabilities.

Determination of what's par in terms of an average collection for a company is somewhat difficult. It will, of course, fluctuate depending upon the credit terms, that is, on the amount of time the firm allows its customers to pay their bills. If, for example, a company allows sixty days of credit outstanding, then obviously its average collection period will equal sixty days. If, however, as is so commonly the case, thirty days of credit is the normal period of time extended, then anything over thirty days represents a collection period beyond established credit terms. As a practical matter, not all customers pay their bills promptly, so that there will always be some excess over the formal credit terms extended by the company. Clearly, if a company is generous in its extension of credit terms more funds will be required and the liquidity of its receivables will be reduced. The calculation of days sales outstanding can and often is refined by making use of monthly sales data. Thus, the credit sales for the preceding months are added until they reach the amount shown as receivables. For example:

Accounts receivable, December 31, 1971 = $55,000

Credit Sales ($000)

December	November	October	September
25	15	20	30

Accounts receivable must include all of December's sales plus November's sales plus $15,000 of the $20,000 sold in October. This means that days outstanding or the collection period is shown as follows:

Month	*Amount*	*Days*
December	All	31
November	All	30
October	¾	24
		85

The foregoing approach provides a more accurate assessment and is particularly useful in businesses that have a seasonal sales pattern.

Inventory Turnover Ratio

The quick or acid test ratio recognizes the potential liquidity problems in inventories but does nothing to actually analyze them. It simply ignores them. As a practical matter, the liquidity of a company's inventories can be even more important than the liquidity of receivables. To do this, the analyst makes use of the "inventory turnover ratio," which is very similar to the average collection period. It is calculated by using the cost of goods sold from the Income Statement, divided by the average inventory which is obtained from data on this item from the Balance Sheet. The inventory turnover ratio for XYZ Tool Machinery would be calculated in the following manner:

$$\frac{\text{Cost of goods sold for 1971}}{\text{Average inventory year end 1970 and 1971}} = \frac{\$280,000}{(70 + 60)/2}$$

$$= \frac{\$280,000}{65} = 4.3$$

By dividing the average inventory into the cost of sales, we obtain a ratio of 4.3. To interpret this ratio we employ the same logic that we used in the average collection period. If the cost of sales is the total cost that was incurred over a period of one year, 1971, and the average of the inventory at the end of 1970 and 1971 is $65,000, this means that the inventory "turned over" 4.3 times during the year. The company sold its inventory approximately one time every 85 days (365 days divided by 4.3). That is to say, its inventory of $65,000 can be converted to $65,000 of either accounts receivable or cash in a period of a little under three months.

By itself, the inventory turnover ratio indicates how

long it takes a company to liquidate its inventories either into accounts receivable or into cash. Also, a business's inventory turnover ratios can be revealing when they are compared over a period of time. If over this period the inventory turnover ratio declines, that is, if it grows smaller from 4.3 to 4.0 to 3.5, this decrease suggests that the company's product is becoming less salable, portending difficulties for the company. In some situations, a decline in inventory turnover may simply be a reflection of a general economic slowdown with reduced personal consumption.

Many additional ratios can be used to analyze the company's liquidity. The four we've reviewed, however, present the fundamentals. Let's turn next to the analysis of business solvency.

Solvency

The *Random House Dictionary* defines solvency as the "ability to pay all just debts."[3] Under this definition, liquidity and solvency appear to be much the same thing. However, as indicated at the outset of this chapter, we are considering liquidity as the ability to maintain a sound financial position over the short term, and solvency as the ability to maintain a sound financial position over a longer term.

This distinction is more than academic, for a company requires more than short-term capital. In the life of every company, there comes a point when it can no longer finance its operations on the basis of current liabilities.

[3] *Random House Dictionary of the English Language* (New York: Random House, 1968).

When this occurs, it can look either for long-term debt, involving repayment terms of anywhere from five to twenty-five years, or for additional shareholders. Shareholders' equity, which in the case of a corporation involves the issuance of common stock, is almost always totally permanent capital. Long-term debt, on the other hand, must be repaid and also bears an interest cost which, along with principal, must be paid by the business. The most common form of long-term debt is bonds, which appear as long-term liabilities on the Balance Sheet, just above shareholders' equity.

The analysis of corporate solvency involves an examination of the adequacy of the permanent source of capital available to a business. The first and most common ratio used in this evaluation is the so-called debt-equity ratio.

Debt-Equity Ratio

The debt-equity ratio measures the amount of long-term debt in relation to the amount of shareholders' equity that a business has as its permanent capital. This is done by adding the long-term debt and the shareholders' equity to arrive at total permanent capital, and then determining the percentage of each in relationship to the total for the debt-equity ratio. For XYZ Tool Machinery, this would appear as shown below:

Long-term liabilities	$ 70,000
Shareholders' equity	133,000
Total	$203,000

$$\frac{\text{Debt: } \$70,000}{\text{Total debt + shareholders' equity: } \$203,000} = .35$$

The debt-equity ratio of .35 means that 35 cents of every one dollar of permanent capital is long-term debt. Put another way, the shareholders have invested approximately $2 for every $1 of long-term debt in the corporation. The interpretation of the debt-equity ratio obviously becomes somewhat judgmental. We can see, however, that if the debt-equity ratio indicated that the long-term debtors of the company had invested more money than the shareholders, there may be cause for concern about the adequacy of the permanent capital that was available for the company.

A very rough rule of thumb in American business is that a company's debt-equity ratio should not exceed .33. That is to say, it is assumed that over the long term a corporation cannot incur more than $1 of long-term debt for every $3 of permanent capital. Many businesses, of course, do not operate within this particular capital structure. A business with a very high debt-equity ratio or a greater proportion of long-term debt is said to be undercapitalized.

Insufficient permanent capital or undercapitalization can have several adverse consequences. Long-term debt requires repayment, but to assure growth a business must make new investments on a continuing basis. The earnings that can be reinvested are not always sufficient for this purpose. A company with insufficient permanent capital may restrain the growth of its operation.

There is a second way to calculate a debt-equity ratio. Our illustration took the relationship of the long-term liabilities to the total long-term debt and shareholders' equity. An alternate approach is to determine the proportionate relationship between the long-term liabilities and the equity capital. In the case of XYZ Tool Machinery, this would be $70,000 to $133,000, or a ratio of .53. This method gives a higher debt-equity ratio.

A clear understanding of the approach used to calculate the debt-equity ratio is imperative for the proper analysis and interpretation of the ratio. The conventional yardstick of a .33 ratio is based on the calculation using the sum of long-term liabilities and shareholders' equity as the denominator. Also, if a company obtains a disproportionate amount of its permanent capital in the form of long-term debt, it may become burdened with excessively large payments associated with the long-term debt. This particular aspect will now be explored by discussing another ratio associated with solvency, the "times-interest-earned ratio."

Times-Interest-Earned Ratio

Long-term debt may be obtained from a private institution or possibly on the bond market. Whatever the source, however, a fixed annual interest cost is attached to the use of the capital. As a general rule, when a corporation is unable to pay this annual fixed cost, the creditor has a right to demand payment not only of any interest due but also of the principal of the original sum he loaned. For this reason it becomes important for business to be able to meet its fixed annual interest obligations.

The ratio that attempts to qualify the company's ability to do this is called the "times-interest-earned ratio," which is calculated as follows. First, the operating income of the company is obtained from the Income Statement. Second, this figure is divided by the annual interest expense associated with the company's long-term debt to arrive at the times-interest-earned ratio. The annual interest cost can usually be obtained from the Income Statement. However, in some cases it may be necessary to separate the interest cost associated with short-term borrowing from that of long-term borrowing. The times-interest-earned ratio for XYZ Tool Machinery would be calculated this way:

$$\frac{\text{Operating income}}{\text{Interest expense on bonds}} = \frac{\$50,000}{\$4,200} = 11.9$$

From the above, we see that last year the operating profits of the company were 11.9 times greater than the annual amount of interest they would be required to pay on their long-term debt. Therefore, a very significant change in the level of the company's profitability would have to occur before the company's ability to meet its annual interest payment was seriously jeopardized. If, for example, the times-interest-earned ratio were only 1.2 or 1.5, we might begin to worry as to whether the company could meet these fixed annual payments if the business were to be adversely affected by a slowdown in the economy or a dropoff in the sales of a major product.

A technical point here is that the times-interest-earned ratio takes the interest cost before rather than after taxes. This is because the operating profits used in the numerator are profits before taxes, not after. Therefore, to obtain a comparable relationship, the interest costs used in this calculation must also be on a before-tax basis.

Profitability

A corporation may be liquid and solvent. However, unless it is profitable, its liquidity and solvency are probably not too significant. As we said earlier, profitability is the sine qua non of American corporate enterprise. Let's now look at some of the analytical ratios that are used to evaluate profitability.

Net Profit as a Percentage of Sales

One of the most common ways to express corporate profitability is to take the net profit and express it as a percentage of each dollar of sales. In this ratio, annual net income becomes the numerator of the equation, and the total annual net sales becomes the denominator. Net profits as a percentage of sales of XYZ Tool Machinery would be calculated as follows:

$$\frac{\text{Net income after tax}}{\text{Annual sales}} = \frac{\$23,000}{\$400,000} = 5.7$$

This ratio tells us that on every dollar of sales, the company makes a net profit of 5.7 cents.

Gross Margin

Another commonly used measure of profitability is the gross margin as a percentage of sales. Gross margin results from the deduction of cost of goods sold from sales. The calculation is exactly the same as net income to sales except that gross profit is used as the numerator. The gross margin as a percent of sales for the company would be calculated as shown below:

$$\frac{\text{Gross profit}}{\text{Annual sales}} = \frac{\$120,000}{\$400,000} = 30\%$$

The gross margin ratio simply indicates how much the company has in terms of cents per sales dollar which remain to cover the selling and administrative expenses of its operation.

It is obvious that the higher either the gross or net profit is as a percentage of sales, the better. Clearly, it is preferable for a company to make a net income to sales ratio of 10 percent on every sales dollar rather than 5 percent. Likewise, a gross margin of 45 percent is better than a gross margin of 35 percent.

Gross margin or net income ratios, like other financial ratios, become even more meaningful when they are used to evaluate profit results over a period of time. Thus, if an analysis of the last five years of net income as a percentage of sales indicates that the ratio is declining, the business is experiencing a significant and perhaps ominous change. Likewise, a gross margin trend can be highly indicative; it may suggest either that raw material costs are increasing or that manufacturing efficiency is waning.

Gross margin and net income ratios certainly have their place in financial analysis, but they evaluate only profitability. We can't really get a proper perspective until we relate the profitability of venture to the funds that have been invested. For this evaluation, the financial analyst must turn to ratios which measure profits in relation to investment.

Return on Investment

The starting point for a sound analysis of return on investment is a clear definition of that term, since it can mean many things. We need to know, for example, whose investment we are talking about. The shareholders'? All permanent capital? Shareholders' equity, as well as long-term debt? Or perhaps *all* the assets used by the company in its operation?

There are three definitions, and any one of them can be correct, depending on the circumstances.

Return on Shareholders' Investment

"Return on shareholders' investment" is often also called "return on shareholders' equity." It indicates the return that the shareholders enjoy by relating the net income of the business to the investment they originally made in the form of common stock and subsequently in the earnings returned in the business. In this ratio, the numerator is the net income for the period; the denominator is the shareholders' equity. The shareholders' equity can be calculated (1) on the basis of shareholders' equity at the end of the accounting period, and (2) on the basis of the average at the beginning and the end of the accounting period.

Using the first approach, we would calculate the return on shareholders' investment for XYZ Tool Machinery as follows:

$$\frac{\text{Net income}}{\text{Shareholders' equity at December 31, 1971}} = \frac{\$23,000}{\$133,000} = 17\%$$

The return on the shareholders' investment in the company is 17 percent. Compare this with the return of 5 to 6 percent that they could obtain in a savings account. Little risk is involved in investment in a savings account whereas some risk is undoubtedly involved in the investment in common stock (witness the dramatic downturn in corporate profits in the recession of 1970). As a general rule, return correlates with risk; thus, the higher the risk, the greater should be the return.

Although it is useful to think of return in the same context as interest paid on a deposit, we should stress the fact that the amount of cash the shareholder will receive from his investment depends on the dividends that are paid by the company. It is conceivable that those dividends amount to 100 percent of the earnings. However, this is not likely to happen, since almost all businesses reinvest their portion of their earnings back into the business to assure continued growth. The ratio that measures the cash the shareholder receives is the dividend-yield ratio, which will be discussed later.

Return on Total Capital

The second method for determining return on investment is to consider the investment as the total permanent capital of the corporation, including long-term as well as shareholders' equity. Under this formula, all sources of permanent capital are included in the investment. The return on total capital for XYZ Tool Machinery would be calculated as shown in Exhibit 18.

We can see from that illustration that the net income figure used in the ratio is adjusted for the effect of interest expense on that income. Because long-term debt is used as part of the investment denominator in this calculation, the expenses associated with this source of capital are added back to net income so as to avoid a distortion.

The return on total capital for the company is less than the return on shareholders' investment. This is always the case, since the incorporation of long-term debt increases the denominator in a much greater proportion than the increase to the profit numerator as a result of the

Exhibit 18. Return on total investment for XYZ Tool Machinery

Net income after tax	$23,000
Add back interest on long-term debt	
Interest before tax: $4,200	
Tax deduction on interest	
expense at 50%: $2,100	
Interest expense after tax	2,100
Net income after tax adjusted for interest	$25,100
Total capital	
Long-term debt	$ 70,000
Shareholders' equity	133,000
	$203,000

$$\frac{\text{Net income} - \text{interest adjusted}}{\text{Total capital}} = \frac{\$25,100}{\$203,000} = 12.3\%$$

interest adjustment. When return on investment is calculated with total capital as the investment denominator, the resulting figure obviously no longer reflects the return to shareholders. Rather, it represents the return on the total permanent capital of the corporation irrespective of its source. If this approach is used, a more meaningful evaluation of profitability can be made in relation to the total permanent capital of the business, whether it is long-term debt or shareholders' equity.

Assume, for example, that a competitor similar in size and profitability to XYZ Tool Machinery also has a total capital investment of $203,000. However, $100,000 of this amount is in the form of long-term debt, and $103,000 is stockholders' equity. The comparative returns of the two companies are shown in Exhibit 19.

Exhibit 19. Comparative returns on capital.

	XYZ Tool Machinery	*Competitor*
Long-term debt	$ 70,000	$100,000
Shareholders' equity	133,000	103,000
Total capital	$203,000	$203,000
Net income	$ 23,000	$ 22,100
Annual interest expense	4,200	6,000
Annual interest expense adjusted for taxes at 50%	2,100	3,000

Calculation of Return on Shareholders' Investment

$$\frac{\text{Reported net income}}{\text{Shareholders' equity}} = \frac{\$23,000}{\$133,000} \text{ or } \frac{\$22,100}{\$103,000}$$

Percent return on shareholders' equity	17%	21%
Reported net income	$ 23,000	$ 22,100
Add back annual interest expense adjusted for taxes	2,100	3,000
Totals	$ 25,100	$ 25,100

Calculation of Return on Total Capital

$$\frac{\text{Reported net income adjusted for interest expense}}{\text{Total capital}} = \frac{\$25,100}{\$203,000} \text{ or } \frac{\$25,100}{\$203,000}$$

Percent return on total capital	12%	12%

We can see that the return on shareholders' investment is influenced by the makeup of the business's permanent capital. As Exhibit 19 suggests, an evaluation of return made exclusively on the basis of shareholders' investment can be misleading. For this reason many analysts believe that return on total capital is a more accurate indication of the adequacy of management's efforts to obtain an adequate return on investment.

Return on Total Assets

The search for an investment denominator that is unaffected by the makeup of a business's capital leads finally to the calculation of "return on the basis of total assets." Under this approach, the investment denominator is defined as the total assets used by the company to generate its net income, or, to put it another way, the total of all items on the left-hand side of the Balance Sheet. The calculation for return on total assets for XYZ Tool Machinery would be as follows:

Net income after taxes	$23,000
Add back interest expense after income taxes	2,100
Net income adjusted for interest after taxes	$25,100

$$\frac{\$25,100 \text{ (adjusted net income)}}{\$303 \text{ (total assets)}} = 8.3\% \text{ return on total assets}$$

In the calculation of return on total assets, all interest expense on both short- and long-term borrowings are added back to net income on an after-tax basis. The rationale for this adjustment is the same for the return on total capital. When calculated on the basis of total assets, the return for the company is even lower. Here again, the reason is that the investment base has been increased in relation to the profit numerator.

Proponents of the total asset approach to evaluation of ROI argue that the distinction between permanent and short-term capital is fuzzy. They contend that many corporations obtain short-term borrowings and renew them year after year, so that in reality they are de facto forms of permanent capital and that the return can be favorably influenced because such capital is excluded from the investment base. Therefore, they argue that the best way to measure managerial performance is to ignore completely the sources of invested funds and instead to study only the results obtained on the total of all funds invested in the business. The return on total assets, of course, accomplishes this objective and has come into use for just this reason.

Each particular approach to evaluating return on investment has its relevance, depending on the purpose of the analysis. There is not necessarily one best way. Above all, the nonfinancial executive should appreciate the fact that there are several approaches to evaluating return on investment. The results, and more importantly, the conclusions drawn, can vary with the method employed.

Further ROI Analyses

Return on investment is actually a composite of many factors, as Exhibit 20 shows. Although return on investment is expressed as a single result, it is actually dependent upon the interplay of important factors. The first factor is the rate at which the business's investment is turned over. Generally speaking, adequate turnover—the rate at which the assets are used to generate sales revenue—comes from successful sales efforts.

Exhibit 20. Components of return on investment.

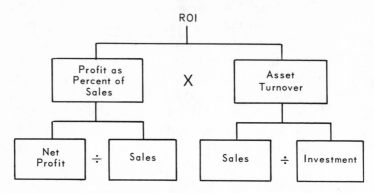

The second factor that influences return on investment is the percentage relationship of net income to each dollar of sales (by itself an analytical ratio reviewed earlier). The net income percent to sales ratio generally depends on the ability of the company to control its costs. Businesses use different combinations of the profit and turnover elements to generate a return on invested funds. In fact, there is an old saying, "Are you in business for fast pennies or slow nickels?" The following table illustrates this particular statement.

	Company A Fast Pennies	Company B Slow Nickels
Sales	$5,000,000	$5,000,000
Net income	50,000	250,000
Investment	500,000	2,500,000
Net income as % sales	1%	5%
Investment turnover	10	2
ROI	1% × 10 = 10%	2% × 5 = 10%

The reader will readily recognize various types of businesses that fit into the two general categories. The local supermarket and dime store are probably classic illustrations of businesses that earn their return in terms of fast pennies; that is, they have a relatively low net income as a percentage of sales, but they turn over their assets many times during the year to generate the return. The marina that we used as an illustration earlier is a good example of the so-called slow nickels approach to generate a return. This type of business has a much higher profit on each dollar of sales but turns over assets much less frequently.

What might be called the "component method" of analyzing return on investment was first used by the Du Pont Company as an integral part of its management control system and has now gained wide acceptance and use in other companies as a management tool.

Financial Analysis: Some Disclaimers

The techniques of financial analysis can be extremely effective instruments for incisive and meaningful interpretations of accounting data. They should always be used, however, with full appreciation of the limitations of the particular accounting data from which they are generated. These have been touched upon at various points in this book, and are included in the considerations below.

Money Only

Accounting measures business results only in terms of money. With this constraint the significant aspects of a business may be overlooked, both in the accounting records and in a financial analysis of them.

History

The past may be prologue, but the chances of this being true in today's dynamic and changing business world are remote. Accounting data is historical. It only tracks where a business has been. Ratios derived from this history beg the really difficult question of where a business is going.

The Cost Concept

Under the cost concept most Balance Sheet values are at cost. Despite its advantages, this particular approach has limitations which grow even more pronounced as the rate of inflation in the United States increases. Accounting data, based on the cost concept, is in a certain sense unrealistic. The ratios developed from this data suffer the same deficiency.

Options

Accounting is much more of an art than a science, an art at least in the sense that much is left to the discretion of the accountant. There are options, however, such as in the choice of LIFO, FIFO, or the Average Method; in methods of depreciation; in estimates of salvage value of fixed assets; and in manufacturing cost methods.

Financial ratios, and all other managerial tools, are an aid to—but not a substitute for—sound business judgment.

Index